New Vic Theatre, Ne·
and Oldham Coliseı

C000077131

by Amanda Whittington

Kiss Me Quickstep was first performed on Friday 4 March 2016
at the New Vic Theatre, Newcastle-under-Lyme

A New Vic Theatre and Oldham Coliseum Theatre production

by Amanda Whittington

CAST

Samantha Shaw	AMY BARNES
Justin Atherton	MATT CROSBY
Nancy Knight	HANNAH EDWARDS
Compère	ALISON HAMMOND
Mick Knight	JACK LORD
Jodie Atherton	ABIGAIL MOORE
Luka Kralj	ISAAC STANMORE
Lee Hart	ED WHITE

COMMUNITY ENSEMBLE
(for Newcastle-under-Lyme)
The Academy for Theatre Arts

Estelle Baddeley	Lewis Jones Dunn
Bethany Bairstow Morris	Molly Joynson
Leoni Barker	Henry Marks
Jessica Bates	William May
David Colclough	Daniel Miller
Charlie Dennis	Lauren Ratty
Joshua Edwards	Joe Readman
Lucy Gough	Georgia Sproston
Lydia Hall	Shannon Webb
Grant Haining	Siobhan Webb
Benjamin Hemmings	Hannah White (Dance Captain)
Lori Hopkinson	Bradley Williamson

CREATIVE TEAM

Director	THERESA HESKINS
Set Designer	DAWN ALLSOP
Choreographer	BEVERLEY EDMUNDS
Lighting Designer	DANIELLA BEATTIE
Musical Supervisor	JAMES ATHERTON
Sound Designers	JAMES EARLS-DAVIS
	ALEX DAY
Assistant Director	CHRISTA HARRIS
Choreographer's Assistant	MARISSA CRAIN
Casting Associate	ANJI CARROLL CDG
Vocal Coach	CAROLINE HETHERINGTON
Company Stage Manager	STRUAN SEWELL
Deputy Stage Manager	STEVE HALL
Assistant Stage Manager	NATALIE HAINON
Technical Assistant Stage Manager	LIAM SHEPHERD

Set and props made by the New Vic Workshop
Costumes by the New Vic Costume Department
Special acknowledgements for costumes: Linda Worrall
Lighting and sound operated by
Daniella Beattie, James Earls-Davis, Peter Morgan and Alex Day

LIFE IN A MIRRORBALL LIGHT

The first step towards *Kiss Me Quickstep* takes me to Blackpool Dance Festival. Held in the gorgeous Winter Gardens, this world-famous competition sees three thousand couples representing sixty countries in ballroom and Latin. If there's a play in competitive dance, then it must be found here.

The world feels completely off-kilter with everyday life but its surreal sights have a strange kind of beauty. Glitz and glamour are everywhere – the frocks, fake tans and fixed smiles – along with the steely eyed stares and sharp elbows of those in it to win.

The dancing, of course, is extraordinary; so are the gowns and tailsuits hung at the back of the ballroom where hundreds of dancers must dress. I don't expect to see backstage in full public view. I snatch photos of dancers in stairwells with suitcases spilling open, making-up and maybe breaking up, too? 'More couples split up at Blackpool than Christmas,' I'll later be told.

One night, I see a young dancer sat on the floor, still in her ball gown and head in her hands. What's her story? Why is she here, tonight, in a world that seems frozen in time? The play will begin with that question.

Later, I meet wonderful dancers who tell me their stories, both on the record and off. I'm indebted to them and to the local dance schools who allowed me into their classes, competitions and confidence. Thank you also to Theatre Writing Partnership, whose *Making Tracks* bursary enabled the first creative journey to Blackpool. Last but not least to Theresa Heskins and the New Vic Theatre for commissioning and believing in the play.

Like ballroom and Blackpool, I daresay there's truth and illusion within *Kiss Me Quickstep*: life caught in a mirrorball light.

Amanda Whittington

CAST AND CREATIVE TEAM

Amy Barnes (SAMANTHA SHAW)
This is Amy's first appearance at the New Vic. Theatre credits include: *Decadence* (Nuffield scratch performance); *Love for Love* (Bristol Old Vic); *Woman & Scarecrow* (Tobacco Factory); *The Merchant of Venice, Alice in Wonderland* (Redgrave, Bristol); *Henry VI Part I* (Rose Bankside); *After the Dance* (National Theatre). Television and film credits include: *Holby City* (BBC); *Mystery Files* (Parthenon). Amy trained at Bristol Old Vic Theatre School, graduating in summer 2015. She recently co-founded her own theatre company, cartilage&drum.

Matt Crosby (JUSTIN ATHERTON)
This is Matt's first appearance at the New Vic. Theatre credits include: *The Marat/Sade* (Old Vic); *Romeo and Juliet* (The Swan, Worcester); *Cider with Rosie* (National Tour); *Pericles* (Cochrane); *Robin Hood* (Minack); *How He Lied to Her Husband* (King's Head); *Hansel and Gretel* (Bolton Octagon); *Of Mice and Men* (The Dukes, Lancaster); *5 Children and It* (Illyria Theatre Company); *A Midsummer Night's Dream* (Redditch Playhouse); *Her Benny* (Liverpool Empire); *Michaelangelo's Slave* (Wimbledon Attic Studio); *Toska* (Monroe, Los Angeles); *As You Like It* (Arts, Hollywood); *Look Back in Anger* (Strasberg Studio, Los Angeles); ten years at the Cambridge Arts Theatre as resident comic and current Dame/co-writer for their annual pantomime. Television and film credits include: *The Levels* (Independent Light Pictures); *Survivors* (HTV); *No Angels* (C4); *Eyes Down* (BBC); *General Hospital* (ABC Television Network, Los Angeles); *The Calcium Kid* (Working Title Pictures). Matt trained at the Bristol Old Vic Theatre School and the Strasberg Institute, Los Angeles.

Hannah Edwards (NANCY KNIGHT)
For the New Vic: *Tale Trail to Robin Hood and Marian, Inherit the Wind, I Don't Want to Set the World on Fire!, The Hundred and One Dalmatians, A Christmas Carol, Alice in Wonderland.* At the New Vic: *She Stoops to Conquer* (Northern Broadsides). Other theatre credits include: *Horniman's Choice* (Finborough); *Romeo and Juliet* (Theatre Royal Bury St Edmunds); *Country Music* (Trafalgar Studios); *Rumpole of the Bailey* (Bath Literary Festival); *Chitty Chitty Bang Bang* (London Palladium). Television and film credits include: *Call the Midwife, Being April* (BBC); *Life Begins* (ITV); *The Priory* (Channel 4); *Alternative Voting* (Great Western Features); *Flowers* (NFTS). Radio credits include: *The Chess Girls*, (BBC Radio 4); *Charley From Outside* (Independent Radio Drama Productions). Hannah trained at Bristol Old Vic Theatre School.

Alison Hammond (COMPÈRE)
This is Alison's first credit for the New Vic. Television appearances and presenting include: *Strictly Come Dancing* series 2014, *MasterChef, BBC Exchange* (BBC); *This Morning* regular presenter and celebrity interviewer, *Big Star, Little Star, I'm a Celebrity... Get Me Out of Here!, Who's Doing the Dishes?, Loose Women, Inside Out* (ITV); *Turn On Terry* (Turn on Production Company); *Big Brother* (Channel 4). Television acting credits include: *Boon, Palace Hill, Yes* (Central); *Dumping Ground, Chalkface, Doctors, Locksmith* (BBC).

Jack Lord (MICK KNIGHT)

At the New Vic: *The Winter's Tale* (Northern Broadsides tour). Other theatre credits include: *Mist in the Mirror* (Oldham Coliseum/national tour); *Rock of Ages* (Ambassador Theatre Group tour); *Accidental Death of an Anarchist* (Oldham Coliseum); *The Jungle Book* (Citizens, Glasgow); *Crime and Punishment* (Citizens, Glasgow, Edinburgh Lyceum and Liverpool Playhouse); *Cooking with Elvis* (Derby); *The Wind in the Willows, Ladies' Night* (West Yorkshire Playhouse); *Midsummer's Night Dream/Macbeth* (Royal Court, Liverpool); *Twelfth Night* (Grosvenor Open Air for Chester Performs); *Our Country's Good* (Original Theatre's No. 1 Tour); *Dick Turpin's Last Ride* (Theatre Royal, Bury St Edmund's/No. 1 Tour); *A Christmas Carol, Grimm Tales, The Glee Club* (The Library); *Ladies' Night* (Royal Court, Liverpool); *Dad's Army* (The Lowry); *Absurd Person Singular* (Bolton Octagon); *Get Carter* (Red Shift Theatre Company); *The Wizard of Oz* (The Lowry and Oxford Playhouse); *Antony and Cleopatra; Pictures of Clay; Major Barbara, Hobson's Choice, A Moon for the Misbegotten, King Lear, Rotten Apple* (Royal Exchange, Manchester). Television and film credits include: *Eternal Law* (Kudos); *Waterloo Road* (Shed Productions); *The Street II, Coronation Street, Cold Feet* (ITV Granada); *Pierrepoint* (Granada Films); *Emmerdale* (ITV Yorkshire); *North Square* (Channel 4). Jack trained at the Arden School of Theatre.

Abigail Moore (JODIE ATHERTON)

This is Abigail's first appearance at the New Vic. Theatre credits include: *Safe House* (Metro-Boulot-Dodo/Wired Aerial UK tour); *Drifters* (Exeter Bike Shed); *The Last Days of Mankind* (Bristol Old Vic); *The Wicked Lady* (Circomedia, Bristol); *A Funny Thing Happened On the Way to the Forum* (Tobacco Factory, Bristol). Abigail trained at Bristol Old Vic Theatre School and at London Contemporary Dance School.

Isaac Stanmore (LUKA KRALJ)

At the New Vic: *Dracula, Robin Hood & Marian.* Other theatre credits include: *Hetty Feather* (original cast, Rose, Kingston/UK tour/Vaudevillem; Olivier Award Nomination for Best Family Show); *Macbeth* (UK and Gulf tour); *Rapunzel* (Lawrence Batley); *As You Like It* (Lord Chamberlain's Men UK Tour); *Wild Oats, Does My Society Look Big In This?, Peter Pan* (Bristol Old Vic); *Knives In Hens* (Greenwich); *Bunkers* (Pleasance); *Phallacy* (King's Head); *White Boy* (NYT/Soho). Readings/Workshops include: *Romeo and Juliet* (Rose, Kingston); *This May Hurt A Bit, Othello* (Bristol Old Vic). Film and Television includes: *The Incredible Adventures of Professor Branestawm* (BBC); *Christmas Angel* (CK Entertainment Ltd); *I Ain't Ever Gonna Gamble* (music video). Radio: *Legsy Get's A Break* (BBC). Isaac trained at the Bristol Old Vic Theatre School.

Ed White (LEE HART)

This is Ed's first appearance at the New Vic. Theatre credits include: *Seven Brides for Seven Brothers* (Regent's Park Open Air); *Guys and Dolls, Chicago, Dirty Dancing, Legally Blonde, Elf* (West End); *Wicked* (UK tour). Television and film credits include: *Penny Dreadful II* (Sky Atlantic); *The IT Crowd* (Talkback); *Mamma Mia! The Movie* (Universal). Ed trained at Arts Educational Schools.

Amanda Whittington (Writer)
Amanda is one of the most widely performed playwrights in the UK. Her plays include: *The Thrill of Love*, which premiered at the New Vic Theatre in 2013. Further theatre credits are *Amateur Girl, Ladies' Day, Ladies Down Under, The Dug Out, Satin 'n' Steel, Bollywood Jane, The Wills's Girls* and *Be My Baby*. She has adapted *Saturday Night and Sunday Morning, My Judy Garland Life* and *Tipping the Velvet* for the stage, and was commissioned in 2015 to write *Miss Johnson* for students at Central School of Speech and Drama. Amanda writes regularly for BBC Radio 4. Recent radio plays include *The All Clear* (Fact to Fiction) and the Children in Need *Woman's Hour* drama *D for Dexter*, which won Best Audio Drama (Series or Serial) at the BBC Audio Drama Awards 2016. Her stage plays have also become a popular choice for amateur, community and school productions across the country.

Theresa Heskins (Director)
For the New Vic: *Robin Hood & Marian, Hoard Festival, Dracula, The Borrowers, Around the World in Eighty Days* (co-production with the Royal Exchange; nominated for Best Show for children and young people, UK Theatre Awards and the Manchester Theatre Awards), *The Hundred and One Dalmatians, Widowers' Houses, A Christmas Carol, Far from the Madding Crowd, Where Have I Been All My Life?, Alice in Wonderland* (nominated for Best Show for Children and Young People, UK Theatre Awards), *The Rivals, The Admirable Crichton, Peter Pan, Bleak House, Humble Boy, The Lion, the Witch and the Wardrobe, The Wicked Lady, A Voyage Round My Father, The Weir, Great Expectations, The Wizard of Oz, Cider With Rosie, Jamaica Inn* and *The Glee Club*. Other credits include: A South Bank Show Award nomination for *White Open Spaces* and an Edinburgh Fringe First Award for *Silent Engine; Strawberry Fields, Precious Bane* (all for Pentabus as Artistic Director); *Grace, Like Candyfloss, Night Train* (Jade); *The Turn of the Screw, The Devil's Only Sleeping* (Birmingham Rep); *Gangsta Rapture, Pink Floyd's The Wall* (Midlands Arts Centre); productions for Custard Factory Theatre, the RSC Fringe Festival, Women and Theatre, the National Theatre Studio, Coventry Belgrade and Soho Theatre. Theresa has written plays and screenplays for the Royal Court Young Writers' Festival, Midlands Arts Centre, ITV and BBC Radio including, most recently, *Woman's Hour* dramatisations of *Lady Audley's Secret* and *Wives and Daughters*; and *The Lion, the Witch and the Wardrobe* has been produced by Northampton Royal and Derngate, Edinburgh Lyceum and Cardiff Sherman. Theresa studied at Oxford University and trained at Birmingham Rep on the ITV/Regional Theatres, Director scheme.

Dawn Allsopp (Designer)
For the New Vic: *Inherit the Wind*. Other credits include: *Dancing Through the Shadows* (Hull Truck); *The Winter's Tale* (Northern Broadsides); *Much Ado About Nothing* (Stafford Festival Shakespeare); *Mrs Warren's Profession* (Cheltenham Everyman and national tour); *Noises Off* (Mercury, Colchester); *Alice* (Theatre in the Quarter); *The Rise and Fall of Little Voice* (Derby Theatre); *Betrayal* (York Theatre Royal); *Midsummer Songs* (New Wolsey); *Drummer Hodge* (Dorchester's sixth community play); *Brassed Off* (York Theatre Royal, Bolton Octagon/The Touring Consortium); *The Grand Gesture, A Government Inspector* (Northern Broadsides);

Ugly Duck (Claybody); *Three Witches, The Night Queen* (Hoopla/Belgrade, Coventry); *Hay Fever* (Oldham Coliseum); *Dangerous Corner* (Salisbury Playhouse); *Sign of the Times, Ballroom Blitz* (Hull Truck); *Private Lives, The League of Youth* (Nottingham Playhouse); *Town* (Theatre Royal Northampton); *Fireflies* (The Lowry). Television credits include: *The Ugly Duckling, Jack and the Beanstalk* (CBeebies).

Beverley Edmunds (Choreographer)
For the New Vic: Choreographer for over thirty New Vic productions including: *Robin Hood & Marian, The Borrowers, Around the World in Eighty Days* (co-production with the Royal Exchange), *I Don't Want to Set the World on Fire!, The Hundred and One Dalmatians, Stones in His Pockets, A Christmas Carol, Where Have I Been All My Life?, Alice in Wonderland, The Rivals, The Admirable Crichton, Peter Pan, Bouncers, The Lion, the Witch and the Wardrobe, Oliver!, Sweeney Todd: the Demon Barber of Fleet Street, Amadeus, Stepping Out, Moll Flanders, Don Giovanni, Pirates on Parade, The Glee Club, Laurel and Hardy, Phoenix from the Flame* (Olympic Torch relay). Other theatre choreography includes: *Geordie Sinatra, A Midsummer Night's Dream, The Mikado, Carmen, Marlene* (Stephen Joseph, Scarborough); *Our Day Out: the Musical, Ladies' Night, Bouncers, Special Measures, Sex and the Suburbs* (Royal Court/national tour); over thirty productions for Oldham Coliseum including: *Hot Stuff, Dreamers, Chicago* (MEN Award winner), *Dick Barton: Special Agent, Stepping Out, Sweet Charity, Blues in the Night, Satin 'n' Steel, Star Crossed, The Rise and Fall of Little Voice, Three Sisters* (Royal Exchange, Manchester); *Song of Singapore* and *Oh! What a Lovely War* (Bolton Octagon); the last eight rock 'n' roll pantos for Liverpool Everyman and Playhouse, *Cinderella, Peter Pan, Aladdin, Dick Whittington* (Liverpool Empire). Tours include: *Lisa's Sex Strike, The Tempest* and *Love's Labour's Lost, A Winter's Tale* (Northern Broadsides); *Return to the Forbidden Planet* (national tour); *A Taste of Honey* and *Carmen* (New Vic and tour); *Sex in Suburbia* (national tour). Film and television credits include: *Disney's New The Evermoor Chronicles, Coronation Street, Hollyoaks,* Children's BBC's *Big Bash, The Agents* (BBC); Fernando Torres's Nike commercial and *O Jerusalem* (feature film).

Daniella Beattie (Lighting Designer)
Training: design and technology at Bretton Hall (University of Leeds). New Vic Theatre as resident Lighting Designer: *Tale Trail to Robin Hood & Marian, Robin Hood & Marian, Seeing the Lights, The Hoard Festival, Dracula, Bell, Book and Candle, The Borrowers, Ghosts, Inherit the Wind, The Hundred and One Dalmatians, Gaslight, Stones in His Pockets, Blonde Bombshells* (with Oldham Coliseum), *The Thrill of Love* (with St. James's), *A Fine Bright Day Today, Alfie* (co-production with New Vic Theatre, Stephen Joseph Theatre and Oldham Coliseum), *Far From the Madding Crowd, Alice in Wonderland, And a Nightingale Sang, The Glass Menagerie* (with Oldham Coliseum), *The Admirable Crichton, Peter Pan, Desire Under the Elms, Bleak House, Copenhagen, Alphabetical Order, The Lion, the Witch and the Wardrobe, Bouncers, The Wicked Lady* (Best Lighting Design at the TMA Awards 2009), *A Taste of Honey, Honeymoon Suite, A Voyage Round My Father, Arabian Nights, Dangerous Corner, Flamingoland, Great Expectations, Laurel and Hardy, Les Liaisons Dangereuses, On Golden Pond, Jamaica Inn, Oliver!, The Prime of Miss Jean Brodie, Stags and Hens, The Safari Party, One Flew Over the*

Cuckoo's Nest, Smoke, A Christmas Carol, Sizwe Banzi is Dead, As You Like It, East Lynne, The Graduate, Kitty and Kate, Pinocchio, To Kill a Mockingbird, Once We Were Mothers, Can't Pay? Won't Pay!, Amadeus, Beauty and the Beast, Kes, Carmen, Once a Catholic, The Lonesome West, Love Me Slender, The Duchess of Malfi, The Marriage of Figaro. Other theatre credits include: The Voyages (Restoke,); Romeo and Juliet, The Tempest (Northern Broadsides); The Mikado (the Orange Tree, Richmond). Installation work: Restoration Agency (touring).

James Atherton (Musical Supervisor)
For the New Vic: Robin Hood & Marian, Hoard Festival, The Borrowers, Around the World in Eighty Days (co-production with the Royal Exchange), The Hundred and One Dalmatians, Stones in His Pockets, A Christmas Carol, Phoenix from the Flames (Olympic Torch Relay); Alice in Wonderland, Peter Pan, The Lion, the Witch and the Wardrobe, The Garden, Don't Turn My Life into a Musical: The Musical. Other theatre as Composer/Musical Director includes: Bedtime Stories (Upswing at Stratford Circus); Eyam (Eyam Church and Oldham Coliseum); The Little Mermaid, Don't Turn My Life into a Musical: The Musical, Alice in Wonderland (Oldham Coliseum); Miss Interpreted (Square Chapel Halifax); Stanley's Stick (Manchester Literature Festival); In My Element (Queen Elizabeth Hall, Oldham); Prom! The Musical, Shades of Grey (Oldham Coliseum); Love and Madness (Barbican, Plymouth); Scheherazade (Bradford Playhouse); According to Brian Haw (Square Chapel, Halifax/Barbican, Plymouth); The Adoration of the Chip (Manchester International Festival). Television as Composer includes: Tales from the National Parks, The Lives of Gandhi, Around the World in 80 Faiths, Olaudah Equiano, Greater Love Hath No Man, Brick Lane (BBC); Survivors, Tonight with Trevor McDonald, Kenny Everett Licence to Laugh (ITV1); The Unseen Eric Morcambe (Channel 4); Roger to the Rescue (Cosgrove Hall); Colleen's Secrets (Channel 5); All in the Game, starring Ray Winstone (Film 4). James is currently developing a new piece fusing his two main loves, running and music. James is also the Artistic Director of the renowned Oldham Theatre Workshop.

James Earls-Davis (Sound Designer)
For the New Vic: all main-house sound designs since 1987 including: Robin Hood & Marian (with Alex Day), Seeing the Lights, The Hoard Festival, The Ladykillers, Dracula (with Alex Day), The Borrowers, Ghosts, A History of Falling Things, Around the World in Eighty Days, Inherit the Wind, I Don't Want to Set the World on Fire!, The Memory of Water, The Hundred and One Dalmatians, Stones in His Pockets, Widowers' Houses, The Thrill of Love, Talking Heads, A Christmas Carol, A Bright Fine Day, Far from the Madding Crowd, Where Have I Been All My Life?, Alice in Wonderland, The Glass Menagerie, The Admirable Crichton, Spring and Port Wine, The Rivals, Bus Stop, Peter Pan, Bleak House, Alphabetical Order, Humble Boy, And a Nightingale Sang, The Lion, the Witch and the Wardrobe, Bouncers, The Daughter-in-Law, Dumb Show, A Taste of Honey, Honeymoon Suite, The Price, A Voyage Round My Father, Arabian Nights, The Weir, Dangerous Corner, Flamingoland, Don Giovanni, Great Expectations, Laurel and Hardy, Be My Baby. Original music includes: Bell, Book and Candle, The Thrill of Love, Gaslight, Proof, Desire Under the Elms, Copenhagen, Blue/Orange, Misery, Dealer's Choice, Romeo and Juliet, Broken Glass (solo), Talking Heads, Smoke, Once We Were Mothers, Kes, All That Trouble That We

Had (with Russell Gregory); *The Wicked Lady, Romeo and Juliet, A Fine Bright Day Today* (with Sue Moffat). Other sound design and/or original music includes: *The Game* (Northern Broadsides); *A Number* (Library, Manchester); *These Four Streets* (Birmingham Rep); *Rebecca* and *Frozen* (Theatre by the Lake, Keswick); *King Macbeth, Silent Anger, Homefront,* and *Sticks and Stones* (Reveal Theatre Co); *Twelfth Night* (Belgrade, Coventry); *Her Big Chance* (Harrogate); several sound designs and/or original music for New Vic Borderlines and Education projects, and soundtracks for community arts projects and films.

Alex Day (Co-Sound Designer)

For the New Vic: *Robin Hood & Marian, Dracula,* Associate Sound Designer on *Around the world in 80 days.* Alex trained at the School of Sound Recording, Manchester, specializing in studio engineering. He joined the New Vic in 2013.

Christa Harris (Assistant Director)

Christa was the recipient of the Leverhulme Arts Scholarship with the JMK Trust in 2015. She has undergone training with Tamasha Developing Artists on their production of *Blood,* and was mentored by Michael Buffong (of Talawa) for Actorshop's *New Visions.* Directing credits include: *Of Mice and Men* (TIE tour, West Midlands); *Dramatic Acts* (Birmingham Young REP); *Twelfth Night* (RSC Open Stages); *Shakespeare On the Streets* (Theatre Absolute, Shoot Festival); *Brick – Where Are You* (The Door, Birmingham REP); *Secrets* (Hackney Empire). Assistant director credits include: *Only on Sundays, The Lion, the Witch and the Wardrobe* (Birmingham REP); *A Third* (Finborough).

Anji Carroll (Casting Associate)

For the New Vic: *Tale Trail to Robin Hood & Marian, Robin Hood & Marian, Seeing the Lights, The Hoard Festival, Ladykillers, Dracula, Bell, Book and Candle, The Borrowers, Ghosts, A History of Falling Things, Around the World in Eighty Days, Inherit the Wind, I Don't Want to Set the World on Fire!, The Memory of Water, The Hundred and One Dalmatians, Stones in His Pockets, Widowers' Houses, The Thrill of Love, Talking Heads, A Christmas Carol, The Widowing of Mrs Holroyd, A Bright Fine Day, Far from the Madding Crowd, Where Have I Been All My Life?, Alice in Wonderland, The Glass Menagerie, The Admirable Crichton, Spring and Port Wine, Proof, The Rivals, Bus Stop, Peter Pan, Desire Under the Elms, Copenhagen, Bleak House, Dumb Show, Honeymoon Suite.* Other theatre credits include: *Judgement Day* (The Print Room); *Precious Little Talent* (Trafalgar Studios; Best Play at the London Theatre Festival Awards 2011); *Othello, Richard III* (Ludlow Festival); *The Ladykillers, Twelfth Night, The Deep Blue Sea, Macbeth* and *The Notebook of Trigorin* (Northcott) and *The Wizard of Oz, Who's Afraid of Virginia Woolf?, Antigone, The Beggar's Opera, A Chorus of Disapproval, Henry IV, Parts One and Two, The Wind in the Willows, Betrayal* (Bristol Old Vic). Television includes: *Inside the Titanic* (Channel 5); BBC2's comedy drama series *The Cup; The Bill* (over fifty episodes); *The Sarah Jane Adventures – Invasion of the Bane;* two series of *London's Burning* (thirty-two episodes), *The Knock* (four 90-minute episodes). Other credits include: feature film: *Papadopoulos & Sons, West Is West, Mrs Ratcliffe's Revolution, Out of Depth* and *The Jolly Boys' Last Stand;* drama-documentary 'Curiosity' *What Sank Titanic?, Mayday, Joan of Arc,* and BBC Radio 4 political drama series *Number 10.* Anji is a member of the Casting Directors' Guild of Great Britain.

Caroline Hetherington (Vocal Coach)

Caroline trained at Rose Bruford College and worked as an actress for many years including a European tour of Howard Barker's *Ursula: Fear of the Estuary* with The Wrestling School and a physical theatre tour of *A Midsummer Night's Dream* with six actors playing all the parts. She graduated from the MA Voice Studies at Central School of Speech and Drama in 2003 and has taught at many drama schools including LAMDA, Guildhall, East 15, University of Minnesota, Birmingham School of Acting, MMU and LIPA. She works in theatres across the country, on location for television and film, and privately with actors, ESL speakers and business people. She is currently writing a book on NW accents, in the *How to do Accents* series, published by Oberon. Theatre credits include: *Hidden* (Black Toffee); *Laughton, Boston Marriage, Sizwe Banzi is Dead, Pirates of Penzance, Moonlight and Magnolias* (Stephen Joseph, Scarborough); *The Guinea Pig Club, The End of Desire, To Kill a Mockingbird* (York Theatre Royal); *We Love You City* (Belgrade); *Dracula, Memory of Water, Dangerous Corner, Don Giovanni, 101 Dalmatians, Laurel & Hardy, Cider with Rosie* (New Vic); *Quicksand, Of Mice and Men* (Dukes Playhouse); *The Bogus Woman* (Keswick Theatre By the Lake); *Whiter than Snow* (Graeae); *The Sunshine Boys, Heaven Spot, Two, Women on the Verge of HRT* (Oldham Coliseum); *Crocodile Seeking Refuge* (Ice and Fire Theatre Company); *The Good Person of Setzuan* (New Generation Arts Festival). Television credits include: *Rockets Island* (CBBC); *There's Something About Miriam* (Brighter Pictures, Sky One).

NEW VIC THEATRE

NEW VIC THEATRE

The New Vic is the producing theatre for Staffordshire and Stoke-on-Trent. Under Artistic Director, Theresa Heskins, our mission is to make excellent theatre-in-the-round, and to be a force for positive change in our region.

Our home was the first purpose-built theatre-in-the-round in the whole of Europe.

With nine major productions a year, we present a varied and adventurous programme that includes contemporary drama, new commissions, innovative adaptations and accessible classics.

We make theatre in an area of significant social and economic disadvantage, but it is an area where arts and culture are making a vital contribution to improving aspiration and attainment and we are proud to be at the forefront of this.

Indeed, this is a creative area where culture is flourishing: audiences in the last few years have been the highest in our fifty-year history; we recently transferred our first productions to London and Manchester; we have a three-year relationship with the RSC's Learning and Performance Network; we were the first building-based affiliate company of the National Theatre Studio; recent work has received UK Theatre and Manchester Theatre awards and nominations. And we lead Appetite, a major audience development programme which, in three years, has attracted audiences of more than 300,000 – in an area with previously some of the highest numbers of non-arts attenders.

We've developed extensive and award-winning community involvement through an Education Department working within the formal education sector and ground-breaking New Vic *Borderlines* working within the social sector, including recent collaborations with the Home Office, the Foreign and Commonwealth Office and the British Council.

www.newvictheatre.org.uk

The New Vic would like to thank all our wonderful New Vic Patrons, Patrons Circle and Anniversary Patrons, we are immensely grateful for all your generous support.

BOARD OF TRUSTEES: Colin Barcroft, Bryan Carnes MBE (Chair), Rosy Crehan, Ann Fisher, Cllr Terence Follows, Michael Holt, Susan Honeyands, Iona Jones, Chris Lewis, Cllr Ian Parry, John Sambrook, Jonathan Shepherd, Cllr Elizabeth Shenton, Sara Williams

NEW VIC STAFF

Artistic Director Theresa Heskins
Executive Director Fiona Wallace

Financial Controller Sarah Townshend
Finance & Payroll Officer Tina Pardoe
Finance Officer Wendy Knobbs
Finance Assistant Andrea Woodvine

Administration Manager Tracey Wainwright
Administration Officer Martin Hayward
Administration Assistant Amy Richards

Head of Fundraising and Development
Michelle Friel-Martin
Fundraising and Events Assistant Paula McArdle
Fundraising Officer (casual) Victoria Martin

Appetite Project Director Karl Greenwood
New Vic & Appetite Creative Producer Gemma Thomas
Appetite Project Officer Katharine Boon

Production Manager Steve O'Brien
Company Stage Manager Struan Sewell
Deputy Stage Manager and IT Officer Steve Hall
Deputy Stage Manager Kate Wilcock

Assistant Stage Managers Natalie Hainon,
Helen Slevin, Stephanie Proctor
Technical ASM Liam Shepherd

Head of Technical Dept/Sound Designer
James Earls-Davis
Chief Electrician and Resident Lighting Designer Daniella Beattie
Deputy Chief Electrician Peter Morgan
Sound and Lighting Technician Alex Day
Technical Temporary staff Antony Clowes,
Ed Costello, Matthew Dean, Beth Earls Davis,
Sam Eccles, Matthew Jones, Patrick O'Brien,
Barnaby O'Brien, Daniel Redfern, Craig Sands,
Paul Willstead

Head of Design Lis Evans
Head of Workshop Laura Clarkson
Master Carpenter/ Deputy Head of Workshops
Lee Wood
Scenic Artist Denise Sewell
Props and Setting Maker Melissa McCann
Trainee Production Carpenter Adam Sutton

Costume Supervisor David Thorne
Deputy Costume Supervisor/Cutter
Sarah Thorne
Costume Cutters Karen Norcross-Downs,
Alison Sunnuck
Costume Technicians Deborah Hall,
Christina Whitehill
Wigs Mistress Eileen Spong
Casual Costume Maker Jayne Lindley,
Charlotte Kazmeriow

Maintenance Technician Mike Unwin
Gardener Ron Gray
Maintenance Assistant Rory Evans

Head of Marketing and Business Development
John Morton
Marketing Manager and Graphic Designer
Candida Kelsall
Press Officer and Online Editor Claire Walker
Marketing Officer Kay Wilson
Web and Graphic Designer Kevin Hegarty
Box Office, Campaigns and IT Manager
Pete Leverett
Deputy Box Office Manager Mandy Fletcher
Group Bookings Organiser Lyndsay Wood
Sales Officers Elizabeth Owen,
Emma Christopher, Claire Wolley
Casual Sales Officer Louise Clarke

Borderlines Director Susan Moffat
Outreach Stage and Technical Manager
Rachel Reddihough

Community Animateur Julianna Skarzynska
Young People's Theatre Company Director and Practitioner Pippa Church
Community Arts Practitioner Brendan Davies
Administrative Assistant Adhia Mahmood

Head of Education Jill Rezzano
Education Administration and Project Manager
Lynn Parry
Education Theatre Practitioner Sarah Richardson
Youth Theatre Director and Education Practitioner Katherine Hughes
Drama Club Practitioner Samantha Vaughan
Chaperones Mary Keogh, Gill Pollard,
Maureen Vickers

Front of House Manager David Sunnuck
Deputy Front of House Manager
Johanna Thomson
Duty Managers Emma Christopher, Mandy Fletcher
Theatre Attendants Emma Christopher,
Mandy Clarke, Maureen Cuell, Barbara Hargreaves,
Angela James, Pauline Johnson, David Kirk, Dorothy
Roche, Roy Smith, Gwynneth Stirland, Nicola Stones,
Joyce Watson, Irene Wilkes
Senior Theatre Premises and Fire Warden
Paula Middleton
Theatre Premises and Fire Warden
Pauline Cregg, Alex Matthews, Philip Stanworth

Head of Housekeeping Elaine Caldwell
Cleaners Debra Bloor, Maureen Kimberly,
Craig McLaughlin, Barbara Wickes

Car Park Attendants Brendan Davies,
Russell Gregory, Paul James, Matt Jones, Antony Lane,
Alex Matthews, Ricardio Sentulio

Catering Manager Pauline Bentley
Chef Paul Dickens
Assistant Chef/Supervisor Roger Hall
Senior Catering Assistant Paula Prince
Catering Assistants Casey Fradley, Jessica Gibson,
Lewis Gibson, Clair Hammersley, Calum Hassall,
Tom James, Pam Jones, Rebecca Jones, Harry Lovatt,
Jessica Stanyer, Pat Whimpanny
Kitchen Cleaner Craig McLaughlin
Casual Catering Cleaner Scott Elliott

Bar Supervisor Rob Punshon
Assistant Bar Supervisor Jamie Barlow
Bar Staff Harriet Barlow, Rebecca Charlesworth,
Lorna Denny, Beth Earls-Davis, Louise Eltringham,
Sue English, Debra Hughes, Kathy Jackson,
Alex Matthews, Alison Podmore, Maureen Rooney

Assisted Performances
Audio Describers Pam Beech, Brenda Hennessey,
Judy Tindall, Tracey Wainwright
Captioners Pete Leverett, David Sunnuck

The New Vic gratefully acknowledges the time and
assistance given generously by the New Vic
Front-of-House Volunteers.

The Academy for Theatre Arts
Principal Jill Clewes
Director Philip Alcock
Finance and Marketing Director Jason McGill
Course Director Lucy Evans
Dance Tuition for the Jill Clewes Academy for Theatre Arts Joanna Lee Martin
Costumes Sindy Crabtree, Cheryl White

Thanks to: Dr Sally Walsh

Coliseum OLDHAM
THEATRE

'For an example of a vibrant regional theatre punching above its weight, you need look no further' *Guardian*

Oldham Coliseum Theatre's history dates back to 1885 when it was one of a dozen theatres in the town. Over 130 years after its first opening, and following two renovations, as Oldham Repertory Theatre and Oldham Coliseum Theatre, it is now the only surviving professional producing theatre in Oldham and one of the oldest theatres still in operation in Britain today.

Under Artistic Director, Kevin Shaw, the theatre produces eight in-house shows a year with its repertoire drawn mainly from plays written in the twentieth and twenty-first centuries and new commissions, encouraging a flourishing community of new writers. 2015's new musical, *Dreamers*, by Cathy Crabb and Lindsay Williams, with composer Carol Donaldson, achieved four stars in the *Guardian*. The theatre's commitment to new writing includes a studio programme under the direction of Chris Lawson, Associate Director, who joined the theatre from London's Almeida. The theatre presents a range of productions from visiting companies, including the critically acclaimed Northern Broadsides, one-night events for music and comedy fans and a dedicated programme for the town's Asian community, including Alchemy, a project with London's Southbank Centre, in 2015. A focal point for the social and economic regeneration of Oldham, the theatre's Learning and Education Department (LED) offers an extensive range of creative activities for all ages, working within the community and providing opportunities for local people to achieve their creative potential.

Recent years have seen the Coliseum flourish with a national tour of *The Hound of the Baskervilles*, working with innovative theatre design specialists imitating the dog in 2012; a *Guardian* four-star reviewed production of *Chicago* in 2013; the 2014/15 pantomime, *Aladdin*, which broke all records with audiences of over 34,000; and the world premiere of Susan Hill's *The Mist in the Mirror* with imitating the dog, which toured nationally to nine venues and was nominated for a prestigious UK Theatre Award in 2015. The Coliseum's co-production with the New Vic Theatre, *Our Gracie*, a new play by Philip Goulding on the life of Dame Gracie Fields, opens on 6 April at the New Vic.

Oldham Coliseum Theatre, Fairbottom Street, Oldham, OL1 3SW
Box Office: 0161 624 2829
www.coliseum.org.uk

OLDHAM COLISEUM STAFF

Directors
Chief Executive & Artistic Director
Kevin Shaw
Executive Director **David Martin**

Board Members
Chair **Gail Richards, Kashif Ashraf,**
Jayne L Clarke, Peter Crowther,
Lynne Farnell, Anne Goldsmith,
David Gray, Cllr Derek Heffernan,
Michael Holt, Cllr Bernard Judge,
Atul Patel, Cllr Bernard Sharp,
Cllr Graham Shuttleworth,
Simon Whitehead, Susan Wildman

Senior Management Team
Head of Customer Services
Liz Cunningham
Head of Finance **Peter Wakefield**
Head of Marketing and Communications
Sue Fletcher
Head of Production **Lesley Chenery**
Head of Learning and Engagement
Carly Henderson

Administration
Administrator **Anne-Louise Jones**
Finance and HR Administrator
Marlene Winterbottom
Admin Assistant **Rose Sergent**

Box Office
Sales and Box Office Manager **David Salkeld**
Deputy Box Office Manager
Ann-Marie Mason
Box Office Assistants **Anna Hughes,**
Anne Mellor, Carol Moore,
Glenda Totten

Development
Development Manager **John Edwards**

Learning and Engagement Department
Associate Director **Chris Lawson**
Learning and Engagement Officer
Chelsea Morgan
Teaching Theatre Practitioner
Liam Whittaker
Youth Board Reps **James Butler,**
Bradley Simms

Electrics
Chief LX **Lorna Munden**
Deputy Chief LX **Jane Barrek**
Assistant LX **Mike Clarke**

Front of House
House Manager **David Rustidge**
Deputy House Manager **Jenny Owen**
Bar and Events Manager **Brenda Lomas**
Deputy Bar and Events Manager **David Carr**
Bar Supervisor **Graeme Gibson**
Bar Staff **Molly Burke, Sean Connolly,**
Millie Cunliffe, Joe Dawson,
Tammy Garrod, Rachel Hollister,
Anne-Louise Jones, Jenny Owen,
Lydia Rainford, Ewan Reddyoff,
Karen Shuttleworth, Catherine Tonge,
Jenny Unwin, Deborah Ward

Housekeeping
Cleaning Manager **Frances Barber**
Housekeepers **Sue Dalton, Margaret**
Barber
Maintenance Technician **Mark Beswick**

Marketing
Marketing and Digital Officer **Ben Baughan**
Communications Officer **Shelly Ramsdale**
Marketing Assistant (voluntary) **Fay Hough**

Stage Department
Technical Stage Manager **Adam Gent**
Stage Technician **Kevin Leach**

Stage Management
Stage Manager **Jane Newbury-Jones**
Deputy Stage Managers **Caroline Bowen,**
Emma Cook
Stage Management Student Placement **Poppy**
Howarth

Wardrobe
Wardrobe Supervisor **Bridget Bartley**
Deputy Wardrobe Supervisor **Janet Weston**
Wardrobe Assistants **Kathryn Ogden,**
Donna Allen

Volunteers
Lynn Ashton, Kieron Ashworth, Chris
Barratt, Aileen Beesley, Joseph Bell,
Lesley Berry, Michaela Bilynskyj, Lily
Bimson, Anthony Buckley, Eileen
Cartner, Barbara Chadwick, Sheila
Chalk, Julie Charlesworth
Mary Cochrane, Philip Diamond, Conor
Fairley, Andrew Fitton, Ann Freakley,
Jean Gamson, Mary Grainger, David
Gibbons, Donna Greer, Barbara Grundy,
Brendan Ivers, Sonia Harrison, Doreen
Hewson
Chris Hook, Marguerite Hough, Jana
James, Viki Langfield, Alison Large,
Miriam Makin, Mary Malone, Gary
Marsh, Alan Parker, Jennifer Parker,
Mary Pritchard, Robert Seal, Paul
Seavers, Judith Seville, Leslin Simmons,
Barbara Smith, Frank Smith, Dawn
Spencer, Denise Swallow, Iain Sykes,
Frank Symon, Hazel Tetlow, Sue Thorp,
Martin Tierney, Marie Tweedale, Thomas
Walker, Luke Welsh, Kyle Wilcock, Beryl
Williamson
Beryl Willis, Theresa Wroe

To join our enthusiastic team of Front Of
House volunteers please contact David
Rustidge on
0161 785 7021 or email foh@coliseum.org.uk

Box Office: 0161 624 2829
www.coliseum.org.uk

KISS ME QUICKSTEP

Amanda Whittington

Characters

in order of appearance

LUKA KRALJ, *a dancer from Moscow, mid-twenties*
NANCY KNIGHT, *a dancer from Blackpool, early twenties*

MICK KNIGHT, *Nancy's father, also from Blackpool,*
    mid-forties

JUSTIN ATHERTON, *a dancer from Burslem, Stoke-on-Trent,*
    early thirties
JODIE ATHERTON, *a dancer from Burslem, late twenties*

LEE HART, *a dancer from Chester, mid-twenties*
SAMANTHA SHAW, *a dancer, originally from Burslem,*
    mid-twenties

We also hear the voice of a COMPÈRE *over the PA.*

*This text went to press before the end of rehearsals and so may
differ slightly from the play as performed.*

A Note on the Dancing

Dance sequences and dialogue may be adapted to fit the performer's level of ability. For confident dancers, the play can be staged as written but simpler routines could be devised for the less experienced.

Act One, Scene Thirteen may be shortened and/or feature the waltz, quickstep and tango only. Act Two, Scene Twelve can also be shortened, and steps for the cha-cha-cha and samba simplified. Alternatively, the competitions could be staged with one ballroom and Latin dance only. Steps for those dances could be repeated throughout the play.

When dialogue refers to the dance steps of individual routines, companies may adapt those lines with reference to their own choreography. All steps and routines are open to interpretation but the storytelling aspects of the dance sequences must remain.

As our characters proceed through the championship, a dance chorus may share the space and augment the competition.

A.W.

ACT ONE

Scene One

*British Amateur Dance Championships. Empress Ballroom,
Winter Gardens, Blackpool. A Friday afternoon in winter.
Present day.*

LUKA KRALJ *enters. He wears a tracksuit and carries a
rucksack and a suit in a cover. He looks around in awe and
wonder.*

LUKA. Blackpool...

> LUKA *goes onto the dance floor. He tries a progressive
> chassé and repeats it with great concentration, his arms
> placed as if dancing with a partner. No music plays but the
> silence gives* LUKA's *steps a compelling beauty. He moves
> slow-quick-quick-slow-slow; slow-quick-quick-slow-slow.*

> *As* LUKA *progresses,* DANCERS *and their* SUPPORTERS
> *come into the ballroom, costumes in hand, excited and
> nervous in equal measure.*

> *Among them is* NANCY KNIGHT. *She wears a tracksuit
> and is made-up to the nines, with hair severely scraped back
> and lacquered.* NANCY *watches* LUKA *before stepping
> forward.*

NANCY. You're here.

> LUKA *stops dancing.*

LUKA. I was early, I...

NANCY. S'all right.

LUKA. I thought I'd come in and...

NANCY. It's fine.

> LUKA *looks up.*

LUKA. It is.

NANCY. So you found it all right? Cos you know we'd have picked you up from the station?

LUKA. I like to walk.

NANCY. But you're staying tonight at our house?

LUKA. I am.

LUKA *is gazing around.*

NANCY. You like it?

LUKA. The floor… the lights…

NANCY. Chandeliers.

LUKA. Chandeliers…

NANCY. I dreamt once they fell as I danced. Crashed and shattered around me.

LUKA. Like a horror film.

NANCY. Tiny beads under my feet.

LUKA. 'The Evil Dance'. Thriller-style. Billie Jean.

LUKA *moonwalks across the floor.*

NANCY (*laughs*). Luka!

LUKA. I like to walk. Moonwalk!

NANCY. Not here!

LUKA. Though Cab Calloway called it the Buzz.

NANCY. Cab…?

LUKA. And Marcel Marceau? You've seen him walk into the wind?

NANCY. I don't know, I…

LUKA. Michael who?

LUKA *does the routine of walking against the wind.*

NANCY. Wow!

> *Enter* MICK, *pulling a suitcase on wheels. He also carries a ballroom dress in its cover and a camera bag.*

MICK. You found him then?

NANCY. Yes.

MICK. The waif an' stray.

NANCY. Dad…

MICK. She's been waiting outside, son.

LUKA. I make my own way.

MICK. Texting yer.

NANCY. Once, that's all.

MICK. I thought you'd bottled it.

LUKA. Bottled it?

NANCY. Cold feet.

LUKA. I know what it means.

> MICK *finds a corner of the ballroom.*

MICK. Come on, this'll do us.

LUKA. Cold feet? Not me.

> LUKA *does his own hotshoe shuffle.*

MICK (*calls*). Base camp.

LUKA. No way.

MICK. Bring your stuff, sunshine.

> NANCY *looks between* MICK *and* LUKA.

NANCY. Luka?

> LUKA *picks up his rucksack.*

LUKA. Never.

> LUKA *heads for their corner.*

Scene Two

Ballroom. Later that afternoon. Couples from the DANCE
CHORUS *gently warm up. They wear tracksuits but hair and
make-up are competition-ready. We hear the voice of the*
COMPÈRE *over the PA.*

COMPÈRE (*voice-over*). Welcome, one and all, to the
  magnificent setting of the Empress Ballroom, here in the
  beautiful Winter Gardens. In a weekend of spectacular
  competition, you'll be privileged to see the very best of
  British Ballroom and Latin American dancing. We begin at
  five o'clock with the Over-fifties' Ballroom. Until then,
  please enjoy the General Dancing to the marvellous Empress
  Orchestra.

  JODIE ATHERTON *strides in. She is fully made-up and
  aglow with fake tan. She carries a ballroom dress in a cover
  and drags a suitcase.* JUSTIN ATHERTON *follows, with a
  covered suit and sports bag. Both wear tracksuits.*

JUSTIN. Jodie!

JODIE. Here's one, quick.

  JODIE *spies an empty corner and goes to claim the space.*

JUSTIN. Conserve your energies, ey?

JODIE. We've got half an hour.

JUSTIN. Forty-five minutes.

JODIE. Well, that makes all the difference.

JUSTIN. You've done your face.

JODIE. On the bloody hard shoulder.

JUSTIN. All right but we're here now and –

JODIE. No thanks to you.

JUSTIN. As I've said fifty times, when a clutch cable goes, it just goes. You can't see it coming.

JODIE. *You* can't.

JUSTIN. That's right cos I'm not a mechanic and I'm not a clairvoyant.

JODIE. I've got one thing to say to you, Justin. AA.

JUSTIN. That's two things.

JODIE. The company car had all that.

JUSTIN. The company car had air-con and heated seats, Jodie. Times change.

JODIE. Too right. Now we're driving around in a death trap.

JUSTIN. Stop being a diva.

JODIE. We're on the M6 and we grind to a halt. Just like Beyoncé does – not.

JUSTIN. I pulled over.

JODIE. We could have been wiped out.

JUSTIN. We could but we weren't and we got here on time.

JODIE. In a tow truck.

JUSTIN. So let's count our blessings, ey?

JODIE. Lets: two hundred and fifty-five pounds for the rescue; a hundred, at least, for repairs –

JUSTIN. All right!

JODIE. And a taxi to Burslem tonight.

JUSTIN. We don't have to go home.

JODIE. Yes, we do.

JUSTIN. Why? We can find a nice guest house.

JODIE. I don't think so, Justin.

JUSTIN. A posh B&B with a sea view.

JODIE. We can't.

JUSTIN. Full English for breakfast? You'll love that.

JODIE. My dress for tomorrow's at home.

   Beat.

JUSTIN. You're joking?

JODIE. Yeah, look at me. Lol.

JUSTIN. Tell us you're joking? Jodie...

Scene Three

Knight Corner. Continuous. NANCY *and* LUKA *are unpacking costumes and essentials: hairspray, make-up, Brylcreem, shoe brushes and shoes.* MICK *takes* NANCY*'s dress from the cover and hangs it up on a nail.*

MICK. Here she is... eight hundred quid's worth of eye-appeal.

NANCY. Dad, don't be vulgar.

MICK. Ballroom tonight, Latin tomorrow.

NANCY. Who cares what it costs? We're not buying marks from the judge.

MICK. Aren't we? He'll clock you straight off wi' this.

NANCY. If I dance well, let's hope.

MICK. Hope? You're out there with sixty-six couples, you've got to be seen from the off.

NANCY. Sixty-six...

MICK. Competition's a knockout, you won't get a second chance. Don't let 'em throw you off-track. Heavy traffic in round one, you can't always do what you've planned, so...?

MICK *nods to* NANCY, *prompting her.*

NANCY. Be ready to change and adapt.

MICK. You listening, Luke?

LUKA. Luka.

MICK. There's two types of dancers in ballroom: the social dancers and what we call the…

NANCY. Anti-social dancers.

MICK. The couples who'll push you on purpose: 'That's our space you're in.' Don't react, Luke.

NANCY. Luka.

MICK. Don't guard your routine. Rise above it and play to the judges. That's who you dance for, so get in his eyeline. Show him a smile. Show him you want to be seen, right?

NANCY. Right.

Beat.

LUKA. Right.

MICK. The first thing he looks for is timing. You're not on? He's turning away. If you are, it's a snapshot he wants. A picture, a moment in time. He likes what he's seeing, he marks it. He don't, he marks that.

LUKA. Or she.

MICK. Ey?

LUKA. He or she.

MICK. Well, of course, Luke, you'll play to the ladies.

NANCY/LUKA. Luka.

MICK. Thinking together, I like it! So out there, present 'em with all you've got, all at once. Flash! Get it? Give 'em the lot!

Scene Four

Atherton Corner. Continuous. JODIE *and* JUSTIN *are putting on their costumes.* JUSTIN *holds a towel around* JODIE *as she squeezes into her dress.*

JUSTIN. You should have just packed it.

JODIE. Why would I? 'It's cheaper to sleep in us own bed', you said. 'We'll dance ballroom, be home in an hour.'

JUSTIN. Well, perhaps –

JODIE. 'Have a lie-in, a leisurely drive back for the Latin.'

JUSTIN. Perhaps you can borrow a –

JODIE. Borrow?

JUSTIN. Perhaps!

JODIE. Three whole days, I've been at it for this. Three days of acrylics and dyeing and tanning –

JUSTIN. I know.

JODIE. You're a man, you know nowt. You don't have to smother on St. Tropez, stain every towel, every sheet –

JUSTIN. I have to smell it though. I have to share a bed with it.

JODIE. 'It'?

JUSTIN. You.

JODIE. Well, Justin, thank you for that vote of love.

JUSTIN. Dunno why you still do it.

JODIE. I'm half-naked out there in the Latin, I have to.

JUSTIN. Nobody has to do anything, Jodie.

JODIE. Oh, fine. So I'll go out there under the lights, lily-white?

JUSTIN. Might catch on.

JODIE. Tell that to Lee and Samantha. They'd laugh in your face, they'd –

JUSTIN. All right, that's enough.

JODIE. You're dead right it is, when my new dress is hung up a hundred miles –

JUSTIN. Eighty miles –

JODIE. Back down the road. When I've spent six hundred pounds –

JUSTIN. Six hundred? You said it was three.

JODIE. No, I didn't.

JUSTIN. You did.

JODIE. Three, six, what's the difference? I could have gone madder than that, spend a thousand or more.

JUSTIN. Six hundred pounds, second-hand?

JODIE. Pre-loved. One careful owner.

JUSTIN. Jodie...

JODIE. A fat 'un, an' all, it needed a nip and a tuck.

JUSTIN. Why didn't you tell me?

JODIE. Cos I don't go on about everything, do I? On and on and on and on and –

JUSTIN. No? That's five 'ons' and counting.

JODIE. A second-class dress makes a second-class couple.

JUSTIN. We're not second-class.

JODIE. I'd worn my turquoise two years on the trot.

JUSTIN. And what card did you put it on, Visa?

JODIE. The feathers were shedding.

JUSTIN. Yes, Jodie, I know.

JODIE. What's that tone of voice for?

JUSTIN. What tone?

JODIE. 'Yes, Jodie. I know.' Don't you want me to look like a champion?

JUSTIN. Of course I do.

JODIE. Can you say that again like you mean it?

JUSTIN. At this precise moment? Probably not.

Beat.

JODIE. You told me last year that we'd come back here bigger and better.

JUSTIN. We have.

JODIE. You promised me, Justin.

JUSTIN. We've took extra lessons, we've gone training four nights a week. We've done yoga.

JODIE. But what if it isn't enough?

JUSTIN. It will be. 'Today's the first day of the rest of our lives.'

JODIE. And we're still up the creek wi'out –

JUSTIN. Look! I'll go back and get it, all right? First thing in the morning, I'll go.

JODIE. Do you swear? On the Bible?

JUSTIN. Latin's not till tomorrow. We've worked just as hard for tonight.

Beat.

JODIE. What are we doing here, Justin?

Beat.

JUSTIN. What we do. We're doing what we do.

JODIE. Under a stairwell with no friggin' light?

JUSTIN. That's Blackpool.

JODIE. Unless you're Lee and Samantha.

JUSTIN. Jodie, will you stop going on about –

JODIE. I've bought this dress five years ago.

JUSTIN. No one remembers.

JODIE. Exactly. No one at all.

Beat.

JUSTIN. What did Bruce Lee say? 'The successful warrior is the average man, with a laser-like focus.'

JODIE. I'm not a warrior. I'm not a man.

Enter LEE HART *and* SAMANTHA SHAW, *with sponsored luggage and names emblazoned on their tracksuits. As they cross the space,* SAMANTHA *and* JODIE *exchange a glance.*

I'm not Samantha Shaw.

Scene Five

Knight Corner. Early evening. NANCY *wears her ballroom dress covered in a black kimono dressing gown with matching slippers. She puts the final touches to her make-up as* MICK *helps* LUKA *into his tailcoat. Beneath, he wears immaculate black trousers, black braces, white shirt, white bow tie and white cummerbund.*

MICK. Berlin Wall falls, '89. I'm sat there watching it all on the news. There's two lads there, East Germans. Wouldn't have been no more than your age. Reporter says: 'What does this mean to you, lads?' Quick as a flash: 'Ve can go Blackpool.' I think: 'Blackpool?' Reporter says: 'What do you wanna go there for?' And they say?

LUKA. To dance.

MICK. Glasnost.

LUKA. Of course.

MICK. Maggie Thatcher, she stood in this very hall, spoke of it.

NANCY. Dad, we need to warm up?

MICK. Perestroika, the floodgates are open. You come, you dance, you wipe the floor wi' us. Conquer the States. Yep, there's more of your Red Army dancers out there than the Yanks.

NANCY. You can't say that.

MICK. It's true.

NANCY. You can't say Red Army, not now.

MICK. You're all right wi' it, aren't yer, Luke?

NANCY. Luka.

LUKA. I was born in the USSR's dying days.

MICK. Well, let me tell yer, back then –

LUKA. In a time when ballroom was banned.

NANCY. Banned?

LUKA. Too bourgeois, too western. My mother competed but only at night, with curtains closed, music so low she could barely...

NANCY. Hear that, Dad?

MICK. Hold out your arms.

> LUKA *lifts his arms sideways.* MICK *feels across his shoulders and runs his hands down the side of the body, as if frisking him.*

NANCY. Dad –

MICK. Underarms tight... Shoulders, tight enough.

NANCY. And the top line's perfect.

MICK. I wouldn't say that but it fits to the body. No wings. No weapons.

LUKA. No...?

MICK. Old English joke. Yep, you'll do.

> MICK *brushes* LUKA*'s shoulders with a clothes brush.*

LUKA. Thank you.

MICK. All part of the service.

LUKA. I will reimburse you. As soon as –

MICK. Bring us an amateur title. That's all I want in return.

LUKA. Tonight?

MICK. Let's not run away wi' ourselves, son. Three years.

NANCY. Three?

LUKA. Three years, British Champions.

NANCY. Now you're finally here. With your visa.

> MICK *picks up a white card bearing* LUKA *and* NANCY*'s competition number – '60' – and two safety pins.*

MICK. Think you can do it?

LUKA. We can and we will.

MICK. Worth leaving the motherland for, in't it? A partner like Nance?

NANCY. Dad…

MICK. Juvenile champion. Junior champion here, twice.

LUKA. Right height, right build, right leg-length.

MICK. Wi' a pedigree, too. Her granny danced til she dropped.

NANCY. Literally.

MICK. On the floor of the Tower. Just as she'd want it to be.

LUKA. So did you and her mother dance?

MICK. Turn round.

LUKA. Did you dance together?

> LUKA *turns around and* MICK *pins the number on his back.*

MICK. Know what does my head in wi' this? You spend five hundred quid on a handmade suit and put on your number wi' safety pins – ah!

> MICK *nicks himself with the pins.*

NANCY. Dad, you're all fingers and thumbs.

MICK. I tell yer, it's bloody –

NANCY. Come on. Let me. Stand still, Luka.

> NANCY *takes over the pinning operation.*

LUKA. I am.

LUKA *starts body-popping.*

NANCY. Stop it!

LUKA. What?

NANCY. Stop!

LUKA. What do you mean?

NANCY (*laughs*). You're a nightmare!

LUKA. Your worst nightmare!

MICK (*sharply*). Oi! You're not here on your holidays, son.

LUKA *stops body-popping.* NANCY *pins on the number in silence.*

NANCY. There, Number 60. You're done.

MICK. So the plan is –

LUKA *turns and looks at* NANCY.

LUKA. Thank you.

NANCY. It's fine.

LUKA. I know.

MICK. Round one: the plan is to go out and dance your routines. Simple as.

NANCY *turns away from* LUKA.

NANCY. Shoes…

MICK. Keep going, keep time, keep focused on footwork. That's what it's all about, ey?

NANCY. Where's my shoes?

MICK. If your feet move the right way, your hips'll move with 'em and then the performance comes in. Luke, you listening?

LUKA. My name is Luka.

MICK. Y'live on the second floor?

LUKA. Huh?

MICK. So when you stand up, stand up straight! And we don't want spaghetti arms neither. Put 'em out, put 'em –

NANCY. Who put them here?

NANCY finds her dance shoes and slips them on.

LUKA. Nancy? Can we talk through the quickstep?

MICK. Don't take little baby steps –

LUKA. Nancy?

NANCY. The quickstep, yes.

MICK. Push off and go for it, right from the start.

LUKA. From the lockstep?

NANCY. Yep.

LUKA. Lock-a-step –

    Slow –

NANCY. Tipsy one –

    Tipsy two –

MICK. You hear me?

LUKA. Full turn, turn, turn –

    Turn and drag –

    And push –

NANCY. And kick and out, kick and out –

LUKA. And swing, swing, swing, swing, swing, swing –

MICK. Nance?

NANCY. Swing round, swing round –

LUKA. Contra-check, and up, and runs, run –

NANCY. And chassé one, chassé two –

MICK. Remembering the floor's your best friend. Staying grounded, keeping –

LUKA (*to* MICK). Excuse me.

MICK. Why? What you done?

LUKA. Nancy and I need to focus.

Beat.

MICK. Fine. Don't mind me. Go ahead.

LUKA *and* NANCY *continue.*

NANCY. Chassé one, chassé two –

MICK. And lock, lock, lock, lock –

LUKA. And slow, wing, slow, wing, slow, wing –

MICK. Not bad, not bad.

LUKA. Again?

MICK. Yep, you do it –

NANCY. Again.

Scene Six

Atherton Corner. Continuous. JUSTIN *wears part of his tailsuit: white shirt, white bow tie, high-waist black trousers and white braces. On his back is the number '22'.* JUSTIN *does warm-up exercises: swinging each leg from the hip like a pendulum; rotating his arms like a windmill; marching across the floor, lifting his knees.*

JODIE *rubs the soles of her shoes with a stiff brush. Like* NANCY, *she wears her ballroom dress with an older kimono dressing gown.*

JUSTIN. Sixty-six couples... sixty-six... sixty-six.

JODIE. How does it help, saying that?

JUSTIN. Psyches you up.

JODIE. Freaks you out.

JUSTIN. 'The journey of a thousand miles begins with a single step.'

   JUSTIN *does a ballroom step.*

JODIE. Who came up with that one?

JUSTIN. Lao Tzu.

JODIE. Chinese.

JUSTIN. Goals: round one.

JODIE. To get to round two.

JUSTIN. We don't have control over that. So my goal in round one is to lead with precision and strength.

JODIE. See you do.

JUSTIN. And yours?

   Beat.

JODIE. To follow as if we are one.

JUSTIN. 'As if'? We *are* one.

JODIE. You can't say 'to follow as one'. Don't make sense.

JUSTIN. 'To be as one as I follow.'

JODIE. Sounds religious.

JUSTIN. You come up with a better one, then.

JODIE. 'As One.'

JUSTIN. That's it?

JODIE. Joint goal. 'As One.'

JUSTIN. Our goal is as one…

JODIE. Our goal is to dance as one.

JUSTIN. Well, yeah. Our goal is to dance as one. One, one, one, one, one.

    JUSTIN *swings his legs.*

JODIE. Do Lee and Samantha have goals, do you think?

JUSTIN. They've a bye to round two, that's all I know.

JODIE. The so-called champions.

JUSTIN. They're not so-called, they are.

JODIE. Up in their own personal dressing room.

JUSTIN. Plugged in and preprogrammed to win.

JODIE. While we're camping out on the floor.

JUSTIN. Little microchips planted inside 'em with –

    As JUSTIN *strides forward, his left knee twinges.*

JODIE. What?

JUSTIN. Nowt.

JODIE. What!

JUSTIN. It's a twinge, that's all

JODIE. Have you strapped it?

JUSTIN. Of course I've strapped it.

JODIE. You've nothing to worry about, then. Have yer?

JUSTIN. No. Nothing.

JODIE. Justin, you knackered it three years ago.

JUSTIN. I did not knacker it. I dislocated the patella.

JODIE. On a slippy dance floor what's nothing like this.

JUSTIN. I realise that but –

JODIE. The physio told us you're better.

JUSTIN. I was. Before I pushed three tonnes of Ford Focus up
    the M6.

JODIE. The hard shoulder.

JUSTIN. Oh, and the difference is…? I still pushed it, didn't I,
    while you sat in the car.

JODIE. Steering.

JUSTIN. Story of our life, is that.

JODIE. You do this every time.

JUSTIN. Do what?

JODIE. The knee thing, last minute, it's some sort of wotsit,
    some psycho-semantic…

JUSTIN. Somatic.

JODIE. Psychotic.

JUSTIN. It still isn't right.

JODIE. Nothing's right, Justin. Nothing.

    Music ends. Applause. We hear the COMPÈRE.

COMPÈRE (*voice-over*). Thank you, adjudicators, thank you, competitors. We continue now with Amateur Ballroom, round one.

JUSTIN. That's us.

> JODIE *takes off her dressing gown.* JUSTIN *puts on the jacket of his tailsuit. Enter* LUKA *and* NANCY, *heading for the dance floor.*

NANCY. Ready?

LUKA. All of my life.

> NANCY *and* LUKA *go towards the dance floor.*

JUSTIN. As one.

JODIE   Where are we sleeping tonight? The South Pier?

JUSTIN. Course not, blimey. The North.

JODIE. You're not funny.

JUSTIN. As one? Jodie?

> JUSTIN *offers* JODIE *his arm.*

JODIE. Book The Imperial, Justin.

JUSTIN. A four-star?

JODIE. Cos I am an Imperial Girl.

> JODIE *takes* JUSTIN's *arm. They exit to the dance floor, shoulders back, smiles wide.*

Scene Seven

*Hart/Shaw Dressing Room. Continuous. The silence between
LEE and SAMANTHA is punctuated by muted music from the
ballroom. The couple are flawless in tailsuit and dress. LEE has
the number '12' pinned to his back. He looks like a 1940s
Hollywood leading man. SAMANTHA has the nervous energy
of a hummingbird. As they move around the space, they create a
ballet of their own. Eventually, LEE speaks.*

LEE. Competitive dancing is not about confidence. It's the
illusion of confidence. And you can create that.

Can't you.

Samantha?

Scene Eight

*Atherton Corner. Later that evening. JUSTIN is half-dressed in
his ballroom suit and JODIE wears a dressing gown over her
dress. They are huddled around JUSTIN's tablet, scrolling
through hotels.*

We hear the COMPÈRE.

COMPÈRE (*voice-over*). And while the judges deliberate their
scores, ladies and gentlemen, we come to one of the
highlights of the evening here in the Winter Gardens: the final
of Latin Formation. As you know, formation is a team dance,
with choreography based on one or a number of styles. So
please welcome, from Doncaster, the Epic School of Dance.

JUSTIN. The Oasis.

JODIE. 'Some Might Say' it looks shite.

JUSTIN. It's en suite.

JODIE. Twin beds. Pink padded headboards.

JUSTIN. You'll not even know in the dark.

JODIE. 'Live Forever'? Not there.

JUSTIN. Telly, hairdryer –

JODIE. 'Morning Glory'? Not.

JUSTIN. All right, there's more here, there's loads more. The Derwent, The Fairway.

JODIE. The Stained Mattress, Ye Old Smell-of-Rot.

JUSTIN. You're a snob, you know that?

JODIE. If you mean I've got standards, then yes. I have and I am.

JUSTIN. There's wifi in that one.

JODIE. There's wifi in Strangeways.

JUSTIN. Is there?

JODIE. Yeah. There's wifi all over.

JUSTIN. They'd all be on porn sites.

JODIE. Justin –

JUSTIN. Or plotting escapes –

JODIE. What are you on about porn for?

JUSTIN. I'm not 'on about', I'm… you started it.

JODIE. What I was trying to say, if you'd let me, is ladies like I should not be expected to sleep in a bed where a DSS dosser has –

JUSTIN. Snob, see?

JODIE. What's wrong with The Hilton?

JUSTIN. It's full.

JODIE. The Imperial in't.

JUSTIN. I've told you, it's eighty-five quid. (*Scrolling.*) Ah, look, The Sea Breeze.

JODIE. Stinks of fish.

JUSTIN. It's been refurbished since last time. Power shower, no headboards, no pets. Looks very Ikea.

JODIE *is looking across the ballroom.*

JODIE. She'll be in The Imperial.

JUSTIN. And there's an offer, too.

JODIE. Samantha.

JUSTIN. Thirty-nine pounds.

JODIE. The Dresden Doll.

JUSTIN. I'll book it, shall I?

JODIE. Deluxe room, sea view.

JUSTIN. We don't want to lose it, do we?

JODIE. We lost it years ago, Justin.

Beat.

JUSTIN. You know what this is? Catastrophisation.

JODIE. It's not.

JUSTIN. It is. You catastrophise everything, all the time.

JODIE. That's cos we are a catastrophe.

JUSTIN. Are we? I've found us a room. In the morning, I'll jump on a train, fetch your dress, come back. Job done.

JODIE. There and back in a morning?

JUSTIN. You're worth it.

JODIE. Am I?

JUSTIN. Just about. One room left.

JODIE. D'you mean that, Justin?

JUSTIN. I do. Special price.

JODIE. I mean about me?

JUSTIN. Shall I book?

JODIE. Justin?

JUSTIN *looks* JODIE *in the eye.*

JUSTIN. If I didn't, I wouldn't be here.

JODIE. No?

JUSTIN. You're my wonderwall, Jodie. So…

JODIE. So –

JUSTIN. Sea Breeze. King-sized bed. You and me.

JUSTIN *taps into his tablet, credit card in hand.* JODIE *watches him, picking her moment to speak.*

JODIE. Justin? What you said about special price… it's a coincidence, that.

JUSTIN. Is it?

JODIE. Cos just after round one when I nipped to the ladies'. I thought I'd cut through to that bit where the stalls are.

JUSTIN. Oh, aye?

JODIE. And you know what it's like, you say to yourself: 'Well, a quick look won't hurt, will it?'

JUSTIN (*distracted*). No.

JODIE. And most of the dresses are way out our league. But. As I was passing, I saw the most beautiful, elegant… turquoise and lemony, feathers all trailed down the back, looks like it's made by a top-class… half-price. I decide to slip it on, just to be sure I weren't missing a steal and Justin, it fit like a glove. So I'm just thinking now, if I got summat from there, it'd

save you the trip. It'd mean we'd go out, guns blazing. The
price what they're asking, we'd sell it on eBay next week for
as much so it really won't cost us at all. So it's actually free.
More than free cos it saves you the train fare –

JUSTIN. Oh.

JODIE. What?

JUSTIN. Nowt.

JODIE. Justin?

JUSTIN. It's nowt.

   JUSTIN *is staring at the tablet.*

JODIE. 'Card declined'?

JUSTIN. Weird.

JODIE. Why?

JUSTIN. You distracted me. I must have...

JODIE. Do it again.

JUSTIN. I will. Yeah, I...

   JUSTIN *is looking from his card to the screen.*

JODIE. Justin? Again.

Scene Nine

Ballroom. Continuous. LEE *and* SAMANTHA *execute practice figures with ease and skill. Their expressions do not give away the nature of the conversation.*

LEE. I do understand.

> LEE *moves* SAMANTHA *into the next figure.*

> I'm sixteen. Gold-medal exam. Step onto the floor and the routine just goes. So I dance the basics. Quite brilliantly, actually. Pass with distinction.

> LEE *moves* SAMANTHA *into the next figure.*

> Then I double – I treble – my practice. Make sure it Never Happens Again.

SAMANTHA. You can never say never.

LEE. I can.

SAMANTHA. But Lee –

LEE. Negative thinking, Samantha.

SAMANTHA. I know, I know.

LEE. Just go out there and follow me. Do what I do, in high heels and backwards. Be what we are. Number One.

SAMANTHA. But it's just –

LEE. Number One.

SAMANTHA. It's just this feeling comes over me. Separation. Like my mind has just sheared away.

LEE. Forget your mind.

SAMANTHA. How?

LEE. Just relax. You're stiff as a board.

SAMANTHA. Lee –

LEE. Relax!

SAMANTHA. Lee, can I go back to the dressing room?

LEE. No.

SAMANTHA. I need to cool down. I need –

LEE. Breathe, Samantha. Just –

SAMANTHA. I need a drink.

    LEE *releases* SAMANTHA.

LEE. Fine.

SAMANTHA. Can I?

LEE. For God's sake, I'm not your...

SAMANTHA. Mother?

LEE. Keeper. Jailer.

SAMANTHA. Mother.

LEE. I didn't say that.

SAMANTHA. You thought it.

LEE. So you're a mind-reader now?

SAMANTHA. As Elaine Paige once said, Lee: 'I know you so well.'

    SAMANTHA *takes a long drink from her water bottle.*

LEE. I know *him* so well.

SAMANTHA. Who?

LEE. She didn't sing 'you' to Barbara Dickson. God. That would have been... (*Pulls a sick-face.*)

SAMANTHA. It's true though, isn't it?

LEE. What?

SAMANTHA. Nothing is so good it lasts eternally. Perfect situations must go –

LEE *takes hold of* SAMANTHA *and pulls her into the steps.*

LEE. Waltz.

SAMANTHA. Lee –

LEE. Brush step and through chassé –

SAMANTHA. You don't have to do this.

LEE. And through chassé –

  Through and hover –

  And back half-a-turn –

  Back, back close –

SAMANTHA. I know the steps.

LEE. Half-brush –

  And turn, turn –

  And over –

SAMANTHA. I've known them for ever.

LEE. Through and –

  Step, kick, ball-change –

  Step-gather –

SAMANTHA. They're all I know.

LEE. Up behind –

  And round –

SAMANTHA. God, they're all I –

LEE. And back-full-turn-and-cross –

  And back-full-turn-and-cross –

  And whisk –

  Chassé.

Scene Ten

Knight Corner. Continuous. LUKA *and* NANCY *are warming up.* MICK *takes a camcorder out of a camera bag and starts to film them. As he does, he gives a running commentary on the action.*

MICK. The tension mounts as we await the results of round one. Here we see how a champion carries himself. Floor presence, even in warm-up, a winner already. A little mechanical, maybe, but hey, so's a Rolls-Royce.

LUKA. Mechanical?

NANCY. Take no notice. I don't.

LUKA. How?

NANCY. Years of practice.

MICK. The gentleman leads and the lady follows...

LUKA. But why is he...?

NANCY. Video diary. He's kept it since I was a kid.

MICK. She moves when he tells her how far, which direction, a rise or rotation. She makes him look good and feel good.

As MICK *comes in closer,* LUKA *plays to the camera.*

LUKA. She does if her body is talking to his... if he invites a response... if they're moving together as equals. Well, when we say equals...

NANCY. Excuse me? I am.

LUKA. She's fifty per cent of the partnership but if he can't relate, she has ninety per cent of the problem.

MICK. Notes from the Little Red Book.

NANCY. You do relate.

LUKA. But we've further and deeper to go. Technically. Artistically. For our judges, our audience, ourselves we must become animal.

NANCY. Animal?

LUKA. Pure instinct, no conscious thought. When we're hungry, we hunt; when we're threatened, we bite.

LUKA goes to bite NANCY on the neck. MICK turns the camera off.

NANCY (*laughs*). Oh!

MICK. All right –

LUKA. Like a caged tiger.

NANCY. Like a laughing hyena.

MICK. All right, that's enough.

LUKA. A proud peacock. 'Look at this beautiful girl in my arms.'

NANCY. Shut up!

MICK. I've told yer, we're not here for laughing and larking about.

LUKA. What is dance, Nancy?

NANCY. This.

NANCY does a dance move.

LUKA. In three words?

NANCY. I'd say... movement to music.

LUKA. Man and woman. Dance is man and woman. And what does a man want?

NANCY. I don't know.

MICK. As I said, the gentleman leads –

LUKA. To put his arms around a woman. To hear music, to sway side to side. To think: 'I want to do this with a little more style, more panache, more seduction.'

NANCY. Seduction?

LUKA *pulls* NANCY *closer to him and dances. His moves become increasingly animal, which* NANCY *responds to.*

LUKA. So the sway becomes foxtrot and rumba...

NANCY. Quickstep and jive.

MICK *watches* NANCY *become more confident in the moves.*

LUKA. But whatever it is, it is always a man and a woman.

NANCY. A man and a woman...

LUKA. In rhythm.

NANCY *is looking into* LUKA*'s eyes.*

MICK. It's feet and legs.

MICK *watches as* LUKA *encourages* NANCY.

LUKA. Yes... yes...

MICK. The more you use your feet and your legs, the more movement you create in ballroom, the more power in Latin –

NANCY. A man and a woman...

LUKA. In rhythm...

NANCY. In rhythm...

LUKA. In rhythm...

MICK *puts the camera into its bag.*

Scene Eleven

Atherton Corner. Continuous. JUSTIN *is still on his tablet, with* JODIE *warming up beside him.*

JUSTIN. I just tapped the number in wrong.

JODIE. Again?

JUSTIN. Bloody keyboard.

JODIE. It's a poor workman blames his tools. Warm up.

JUSTIN. I will. I will…

JUSTIN *is staring at the screen.*

JODIE. Now, please?

JUSTIN. 'Genius,' said Michelangelo, 'is eternal patience.' Think on.

JODIE. Ring your brother.

JUSTIN. What for?

JODIE. Tell him fetch us tonight. We can borrow his car in the morning.

JUSTIN. No.

JODIE. Why not? What else is he doing?

JUSTIN. Job-hunting.

JODIE. On Friday night?

JUSTIN. Yes, as a matter of fact.

JODIE. We can pay him for petrol, if that's what you're worried about?

JUSTIN. How will that help him? The car's gone.

JODIE. It's what?

JUSTIN. He sold it, he had to.

JODIE. You never said owt.

JUSTIN. He don't want people to know.

JODIE. I'm not people.

JUSTIN. It's his business, Jodie. And this is ours.

JUSTIN *throws the tablet in the suitcase.*

JODIE. What's wrong with the card?

JUSTIN. I had to draw cash for the tow truck. It's probably just tipped us, that's all.

JODIE. Over the edge?

JUSTIN. Over the overdraft.

JODIE. How? You extended it.

JUSTIN. Yeah, yeah, tell you what? I'll go to the cashpoint and check.

JODIE. Now?

JUSTIN *is already leaving.*

JUSTIN. It's only outside.

JODIE. We've got to warm up?

JUSTIN. When we've no cash, no cards and no bed for the night?

JODIE. But we'll get to round two, I know it, so come on, let's run through –

JUSTIN *turns, walking backwards and heading towards* MICK*'s camera bag.*

JUSTIN. Don't need to. I've done it before and guess what? I can do it again. I can do it stood on my head, one hand tied behind –

JUSTIN *trips over the bag.*

JODIE. Course you can, Justin! Of course!

LUKA *and* NANCY *run to his aid.*

NANCY. Oh!

JODIE. Bloody Gene Kelly lives!

JUSTIN. I'm all right, I'm –

NANCY. I'm sorry, I'm so –

LUKA. What happened?

JUSTIN. I just got a bit –

NANCY. He tripped on our stuff.

JUSTIN. Honest, I'm all –

LUKA. Let me see.

LUKA *goes to assist* JUSTIN.

JUSTIN. I'm fine. I just need to look where I'm... aaah!

LUKA. Okay...

JODIE. What?

JUSTIN. Nowt.

JODIE. It's not your patella again?

LUKA. Patella?

JUSTIN. I put it out once, that's all.

LUKA. When?

JUSTIN. Years back.

NANCY. I saw you twist when you fell.

JUSTIN. Look, it's only my pride that's been... argh!

JODIE. Tell me no...

JUSTIN. No...

JUSTIN *is clearly in pain*.

JODIE. Justin?

JUSTIN. No!

LUKA *takes charge*.

LUKA. Flex your knee.

JODIE. Well, that's it. We're done.

LUKA. Turn to the right for me.

JODIE. Car trouble, clutch trouble, credit card –

JUSTIN. Jodie!

JODIE. Knackered knee.

NANCY. What's clutch trouble?

LUKA. Good, good. Now turn to the left.

JODIE. An hour and a half on the hard shoulder. Stood in the
pouring down rain.

JUSTIN. It were spittin'. Ignore her, it's barely a – aah!

LUKA. And rest.

JUSTIN. First-aider, are you?

LUKA. I train as a doctor at home.

JUSTIN. How about that, Jo? 'Is there a doctor in the house?'
'Da!'

JODIE. It's a miracle-worker we need. It's a bloody magician.

JODIE *bursts into tears*.

NANCY. Hey, hey, what is it?

JODIE. Everything… everything!

JUSTIN. Stop it.

JODIE. We're out of the comp… on the streets.

JUSTIN. I've told you, I'll sort it.

JODIE. Says you who's gone flying in front of the whole entire dance world.

JUSTIN. He'll sort it.

JODIE. We've nowhere to stay except a bench on the front and I know what you're thinking: 'Well, get a hotel.' But it's, you know, complicated and... Oh, we can't... we just can't...

Enter MICK, *with a pint.*

NANCY. Please don't... your make-up.

JODIE. What good is it now? We're finished. It's over. We're done.

NANCY. You're not. You're staying with us.

MICK. What's going on?

JODIE. You live round here?

NANCY. Three miles away.

JUSTIN. Look, it's dead nice of you but we couldn't.

JODIE. We could.

MICK. Hang about...

NANCY. Dad, it's the right thing to do.

MICK. Did he put you up to this? Karl Marx?

NANCY. It's our fault. Our camera bag. Isn't it, Dad?

MICK. We've got Luke.

LUKA. Luka.

NANCY. We've got six bedrooms.

JODIE. Six?

NANCY. And we'd be delighted to have you.

MICK. But, Nancy –

NANCY. We would. Cos that's what we do here. We're Blackpool.

MICK. Well, strictly speaking, we're Lytham.

NANCY. We're Blackpool.

JUSTIN *stands up, helped by* JODIE.

JUSTIN. We're Burslem.

JODIE. We are.

Scene Twelve

Ballroom. Continuous. LEE *and* SAMANTHA *are waiting to go on.* SAMANTHA *takes a long drink from her bottle of water. His earbuds in,* LEE *is silently preparing.*

SAMANTHA. Lee? Do you know what I think, sometimes? You'll laugh but when I look at all this, I think I've woken up in a fish tank. A gigantic tropical fish tank. A friend from school had one. I used to go round just to see them... going round. Fantail guppies. Black mollies. Tiger barbs. Angelfish. Orange and yellow, neon red. My favourite was pure colbalt blue. So pretty, so very refined. Little schools darting everywhere; zebra danios flitting around. Then you'd look at the angelfish gliding so calmly and notice the barb there behind. She'd nip her, then nip her again. You'd start to see chases. Predators, bullies. Winners and losers and lost little neons.

LEE. What on earth are you talking about?

LEE *takes out his earbuds.*

SAMANTHA. Fish.

LEE. Fish?

SAMANTHA. Tropical fish.

SAMANTHA *takes a long drink from her water bottle.*

LEE. Water goes through you, remember?

SAMANTHA. I'm hot. It helps.

LEE. You don't need help. You just need to breathe on the count.

SAMANTHA. I will.

LEE. One and two and three and four and one and two and three and four and one and two and three and four. Simple as, see?

SAMANTHA. If only.

Beat.

LEE. Samantha, I'm not completely without…

SAMANTHA. What?

LEE. The first Blackpool without her. It's bound to feel…

SAMANTHA. Yes. Yes, it does.

LEE. When she was always so…

SAMANTHA. Yes.

Beat.

LEE. But if you just breathe on the count…

SAMANTHA. What?

LEE. One and two and…

SAMANTHA. Three and… one and two and three and…

LEE. May I?

LEE *opens his hand for* SAMANTHA*'s water bottle.*

SAMANTHA. No.

LEE. Just a sip?

SAMANTHA. I've a cold.

LEE. A cold?

SAMANTHA. Coming on. So, did you have fish as a child, Lee? Tropical fish? Or a goldfish. Any kind? They tell you they're calming but really, the awful behaviour, the fights. No, you're led to believe it's some kind of nirvana but...

LEE. Let the fish go, Samantha. Let all those thoughts float away.

SAMANTHA. How?

LEE. Close your eyes.

SAMANTHA. Now?

SAMANTHA closes her eyes.

LEE. Close your eyes and imagine a cool, calm stream. Imagine your thoughts are leaves on the stream. Drifting by, one by one... drifting away.

LEE grabs the water bottle from SAMANTHA. She opens her eyes.

SAMANTHA. Lee!

LEE drinks from the water bottle and spits out the contents, narrowly missing SAMANTHA's dress.

LEE. I knew it.

SAMANTHA. What?

LEE. I knew it!

LEE grabs hold of her wrist.

SAMANTHA. Let go of me –

LEE. Well?

SAMANTHA. People are looking!

LEE draws her towards him in a hold and starts to dance, fiercely. As he does, LUKA and NANCY, and JUSTIN and JODIE enter the space, psyching themselves up for the competition. MICK follows, a few paces behind.

LEE. What's in it this time?

SAMANTHA. Nothing.

LEE *spins* SAMANTHA *around with menace.*

LEE. Don't lie to me.

SAMANTHA. Water.

LEE. Water and what? What!

SAMANTHA. Just… just a splash from the minibar.

LEE. Splash of what? Vodka?

SAMANTHA. A miniature, that's all. That's all.

LEE *spins* SAMANTHA.

LEE. When you swore to me it was over.

SAMANTHA. It was.

LEE. When you swore on your mother's –

SAMANTHA. I told you, the feelings.

LEE. Feelings!

SAMANTHA. Yes. They're overwhelming.

LEE. Feelings you have and I don't, is that right?

SAMANTHA. Yes. No. What?

LEE. Well, I can't have. I don't need vodka to get on the floor, I just dance on a wave of indifference, don't I? Don't I!

SAMANTHA. I didn't say that.

LEE. No, Samantha. You said that you'd stopped.

COMPÈRE (*voice-over*). Thank you very much, competitors. We continue now with round two of Amateur Ballroom.

SAMANTHA. I can't.

COMPÈRE (*voice-over*). Forty-eight competitors are recalled and they are: number 12, 16, 22 –

JODIE. Yes!

The COMPÈRE*'s numbers continue underneath the dialogue.*

COMPÈRE (*voice-over*). 25, 27, 29, 30, 32, 34, 35, 36, 37, 38, 40, 42, 44, 48, 51, 54, 55, 56, 59...

JUSTIN *offers his arm to* JODIE.

JUSTIN. Here we go.

Exit JUSTIN *and* JODIE *to the dance floor.* MICK *turns to* NANCY.

MICK. The floor's your best friend.

NANCY. I know it is, yes.

MICK. And he might have the moves but he needs you.

NANCY. You what?

MICK. He needs you more than you need him. Way more.

NANCY. He doesn't though, Dad.

MICK. You're a cut above, Nancy. So when he starts calling the shots –

NANCY. He's a man.

MICK. That's incidental.

NANCY. It's not and you know it. For each boy at dance school there's what? Twenty girls?

MICK. You're in a class of your own, Nance. He's still on probation in my book.

NANCY. When you've paid for him to come over?

MICK. Precisely. He's working for me.

NANCY. I don't want to lose him. Not this time. Not after Chris and Gary and Tom and –

MICK. They weren't up to scratch.

NANCY. Who is, in your eyes?

MICK. I beg your pardon?

NANCY. Dad, please? For me, for my future, for...

MICK. What?

NANCY. For the sake of the partnership, please? Behave.

MICK. Behave?

NANCY. Behave.

COMPÈRE (*voice-over*). 60.

LUKA. 60.

MICK. Get in!

    LUKA *puts out his arm to* NANCY.

NANCY. That's us?

LUKA. That's us.

    NANCY *takes his arm.* LUKA *and* NANCY *exit to the dance floor without a backward glance.*

COMPÈRE (*voice-over*). 68, 71, 73, 74, 75, 83, 91.

MICK (*calls*). The floor's your best friend, Nance. The floor and your...

    LEE *gives a hundred-watt smile but looks straight ahead.*

SAMANTHA. Lee?

LEE. Dance.

    LEE *clamps her arm and sweeps her to the dance floor.*

MICK....your dad.

Scene Thirteen

Dance floor. A montage of five ballroom dances: the waltz, foxtrot, tango, quickstep and Viennese waltz.

LEE *and* SAMANTHA, JUSTIN *and* JODIE, LUKA *and* NANCY *take their places. They are joined by the* DANCE CHORUS. *The hushed atmosphere is punctuated with cries of 'Come on, Number 91!' 'Get in, Number 60.'*

COMPÈRE (*voice-over*). Competitors: the waltz.

Music begins. The couples hold one another in a close embrace. The waltz has an elegant simplicity. They dance with a gentle rise and fall, and a lilting rotation.

Your second dance: the foxtrot.

The foxtrot brings a smooth, fluid 'slow, quick-quick, slow'. Dancers cover the floor in graceful trotting steps and zigzags.

The tension mounts with each dance. The DANCE CHORUS *dissolves away to leave our three competing couples.*

Your third dance: the tango.

A European atmosphere sweeps through the ballroom. Military-style drums accompany staccato movements and the couples take clipped, sharp, flat steps.

Your fourth dance, the quickstep.

The light, breezy music of the quickstep evokes the golden age of Hollywood. The couples dance on the balls of their feet, springing the entire length of the space.

And your final dance: the Viennese waltz.

As the montage reaches its climax, JUSTIN *stumbles.*

JODIE. Justin?

JUSTIN. It's me knee.

> LEE *and* SAMANTHA *use nimble footwork to avoid tripping over him.* JUSTIN *straightens up.*

JODIE. All right?

JUSTIN. Yeah.

JODIE. Good.

> JUSTIN *picks up the step but his knee quickly gives way.*

JUSTIN. No…

> JUSTIN *and* JODIE *limp out of the competition.* LUKA *and* NANCY *dance on but* LEE *and* SAMANTHA *command the floor. They execute a cool and graceful Viennese waltz.*

> *The music ends. A triumphant* LEE *presents* SAMANTHA *to the audience. She takes the acclaim but her smile does not reach her eyes.*

> *End of Act One.*

ACT TWO

Scene One

Dance floor. Saturday night. LEE *and* SAMANTHA, JUSTIN *and* JODIE, LUKA *and* NANCY *are competing in the Latin quarter-final.*

COMPÈRE (*voice-over*). And now, ladies and gentlemen, it's the jive!

As LEE *and* SAMANTHA *move centre-stage, the music starts to distort and the lighting takes on a surreal, nightmarish air.*

In response to the music, SAMANTHA *stops dancing.* LEE *stops in time with her, his perma-smile frozen.*

SAMANTHA *stands like a statue in a hurricane as the dancers move around them.*

We hear the COMPÈRE *over the PA and the scene snaps back to reality. The dance ends. All except* SAMANTHA *leave the floor.*

Thank you, competitors. Thank you, adjudicators. That most energetic jive brings to an end our Amateur Latin quarter-final. General dancing now to our wonderful Empress Orchestra but first, please bear with us as we give a little sweep of the ballroom floor.

SAMANTHA *remains static as a* CLEANER *appears with a brush.*

Scene Two

Atherton Corner. Continuous. JODIE *and* JUSTIN *return to their corner.*

JODIE. She stopped.

JUSTIN. I saw her.

JODIE. Quarter-final. Stone dead.

JUSTIN. It's wrong to revel in other's misfortune.

JODIE. Sorry, can't help it. She stopped.

JUSTIN. There but for grace of God, Jodie. There but for that.

    JUSTIN *flexes his knee.*

JODIE. How is it?

JUSTIN. Holding up.

JODIE. Unlike Samantha.

JUSTIN. Frozen peas and a couple of these.

    JUSTIN *presses two tablets from a packet.*

JODIE. Do you really think you should?

JUSTIN. It's codeine not crack.

JODIE. I mean, what if they're making you drowsy?

JUSTIN. Did I look drowsy out there?

    JUSTIN *knocks back the tablets.*

JODIE. All right, all right! Does the dress…

JUSTIN. I've told you, it's nice.

JODIE. It picks up the lights?

JUSTIN. You're a one-woman Illuminati.

JODIE. In cast-offs.

JUSTIN. It isn't a cast-off.

JODIE. She said I can have it. Not borrow it, have it.

She obviously thinks it's old hat.

JUSTIN. Chuck her some cash if it makes you feel better.

JODIE. I will not, they're loaded.

JUSTIN. They're comfortable, yes.

JODIE. Them taps in the bathroom were gold.

JUSTIN. They were brass.

JODIE. They're gold-plated, at least. Walk-in wardrobe, you saw it. En suite, at her age.

JUSTIN. Would you wanna swap with her?

JODIE. Yes, please.

JUSTIN. With all that going on?

Beat.

JODIE. Maybe not.

JUSTIN. I don't think I've ever seen –

JODIE. Nor me.

JUSTIN. It's –

JODIE. Weird. I couldn't sleep a wink.

JUSTIN. So who was that snoring?

JODIE. Not me. Not wi' them photos on every square inch.

JUSTIN. Nancy at three, Nancy at four, Nancy at five-and-three-quarters.

JODIE. Nancy with Artem, with Vincent, with Anton.

JUSTIN. The spare room, the lounge, the hallway, the bog. All right, we've got stuff up, but blimey...

JODIE. It's like a museum.

JUSTIN. A shrine.

JODIE. Them framed little dresses.

JUSTIN. Shoes in glass cases.

JODIE. You don't expect that kind of thing from a man.

JUSTIN. From a dad.

JODIE. And the mother? Where's she?

JUSTIN. Up in the attic, I reckon. Like one of them hermits?

JODIE. Jane Eyre?

JUSTIN. That's her.

JODIE. With great big long toenails and hair down to here.

JUSTIN. And a dusty old ballroom gown trailing the floor. (*As Norma Desmond.*) 'I am big. It's the dance floors got small.'

JODIE. She's the pink elephant in the room, in't she?

JUSTIN. Why pink?

JODIE. I says to Luka: 'You need to find out what's gone off there, and sharpish.'

JUSTIN. It's probably a common-or-garden divorce.

JODIE. Or she's under the patio.

JUSTIN. Could be? Who knows what goes on in a marriage?

Beat.

JODIE. What do you mean by that?

JUSTIN. What I said. Who knows what goes on in a marriage.

JODIE. There's always a double entendre with you, in't there?

JUSTIN. That's not a double –

JODIE. There's always a dig.

JUSTIN. So to speak.

JODIE. See?

JUSTIN. Jodie, we're having a laugh. A little moment of light relief.

JODIE. What do you need relief from?

JUSTIN. You wanna list? I'm tired, I'm aching, I just want to do what we've come for and go home.

JODIE. And how do we do that? You worked it out yet? How do we get from Blackpool to Burslem with no wheels and no friggin' cash?

Beat.

JUSTIN. That couple from Birmingham.

JODIE. Which couple?

JUSTIN. Tina and Kyle, they can drop us.

JODIE. Ask Mick.

JUSTIN. For what? The four-by-four or the Jag?

JODIE. For what we were saying, in bed.

JUSTIN. You were saying.

JODIE. You were agreeing.

JUSTIN. It was two in the morning. I wanted to sleep.

JODIE. Ask him.

Beat.

JUSTIN. I can't. I don't want to.

JODIE. Why not? What's the worst he can say to you, no? You can take that, you've heard it before.

JUSTIN. Thank you.

JODIE. Ask him. He liked you. He might like to help.

Beat.

JUSTIN. I hate all this, Jodie. I hate it.

JODIE. We'll turn it around.

JUSTIN. How? We're twelve thousand pounds in the red.

JODIE. Twelve?

JUSTIN. We've not paid the mortgage for three months now. Three months, you know what that means?

You know what they'll do with the house if we don't –

JODIE. Justin –

JUSTIN. If I don't –

JODIE. Justin! That sign you've hung up on the toilet door? What does it say?

JUSTIN. Does it matter now?

JODIE. What?

Beat.

JUSTIN. 'It always seems impossible until it is done.'

JODIE. And if Nelson Mandela can do it…

JUSTIN. He didn't live in Burslem.

JODIE. Miracles happen. Samantha Shaw stopped. 'Yes, we can.'

Scene Three

Hart/Shaw Dressing Room. Continuous. SAMANTHA *toys with her bottle of water, watched by* LEE.

LEE. How much have you had?

SAMANTHA. I haven't. Not yet. I might not. I just like it with me for…

LEE. How much?

Beat.

SAMANTHA. A few sips, that's all.

LEE. Do you drink every day?

SAMANTHA. Oh, no. No, no, no.

LEE. Every night?

SAMANTHA. No.

LEE. How many nights?

SAMANTHA. I don't know.

LEE. Six, five, four –

SAMANTHA. Probably.

LEE. Four?

SAMANTHA. Five. Maybe six.

LEE. On your own?

SAMANTHA. It just makes it all disappear for a while.

LEE. Always spirits?

SAMANTHA. Look, I don't ask what you do, where you go –

LEE. Always spirits or –

SAMANTHA. What you get up to when –

LEE. Wine?

Beat.

SAMANTHA. Spirits and wine.

LEE. I assume it's been worse since she died?

SAMANTHA. Life? Actually, no.

LEE. Samantha…

SAMANTHA. She's not there, watching me.

LEE. Maybe not but the world is.

SAMANTHA. Unless you believe in –

LEE. Cameraphones, Sam? We'll be all over YouTube by now.

SAMANTHA. Oh, Lee. It's only a dance competition.

LEE. I dance. You go through the motions.

SAMANTHA. That *is* dance. You get up and go through the motions…

LEE. Samantha, we're athletes.

SAMANTHA. For God's sake, it's not like I'm doping.

LEE. You ground to a halt. Like a clockwork toy, like…

SAMANTHA. I did. Maybe I am.

Beat.

LEE. Are you an alcoholic, Samantha?

SAMANTHA. No.

LEE. Isn't that what they all say at first?

SAMANTHA. I'm not that interesting.

LEE. Interesting?

SAMANTHA. No. I'm too thin.

LEE. Physically?

SAMANTHA. Mentally. Spiritually.

LEE. Thin?

SAMANTHA. I feel unreal, quite a lot of the time, Lee. I feel like I don't quite exist.

LEE. Oh, for...

SAMANTHA. I feel transparent.

LEE. How can you be? You've got titles, trophies. You've been on the cover of *Dancing Times*. Twice.

SAMANTHA. That isn't me.

LEE. Who else is it?

SAMANTHA. That's what I need to find out.

Scene Four

Knight Corner. Continuous. NANCY *wears her kimono. She practices a cha-cha-cha.* MICK *is sat apart from her, apparently trying to fix his camcorder but covertly watching her.*

NANCY. Walks –

    Lockstep –

    Walks –

    Lockstep –

    In and hold –

    As LUKA *polishes his shoes, he also watches* NANCY.

    Turn the girl into fan –

    Hockey stick –

    Side basics, New Yorker –

    Hold.

LUKA. New Yorker –

Toe-tap –

Side basics –

NANCY. Practice makes perfect.

LUKA. You want to be perfect?

NANCY. Of course.

LUKA. So where do we find perfection?

NANCY. In the shine of your shoes.

LUKA. In the steps, the figures, the routine?

NANCY. All three.

LUKA. Also?

NANCY. What's this, an interview?

LUKA. Where?

NANCY. Well… like you've said, in the way we relate.

On the floor.

LUKA *steps into the dance. As he does,* MICK *is watching.*

LUKA. Walks –

Lockstep –

Walks –

Lockstep –

NANCY. In and hold.

LUKA. Turn the girl into fan.

NANCY. Sorry.

NANCY *pulls away from* LUKA *and moves across the floor, away from* MICK.

LUKA. Nancy…

NANCY. Sorry. Sorry, sorry, sorry, sorry.

LUKA. For what?

NANCY. You know what. Unless you were so drunk...

LUKA. I kept to water.

NANCY. I wish I had.

LUKA. It's okay.

NANCY. How can it be?

LUKA. It's okay.

   NANCY *glances across to* MICK, *who is just out of earshot*.

NANCY. I thought that's what you wanted. My previous
   partners, they... it was almost expected.

LUKA. Expected?

NANCY. I don't mean I didn't... I liked them, well, most of
   them, Chris was an absolute... oh, Nancy, shut up, shut up!

LUKA. You came to my room, so what?

NANCY. And got into your bed.

LUKA. It's nothing.

NANCY. Well, you made that perfectly –

LUKA. Practice makes perfect, so... walks, lockstep.

   MICK *is watching them*. NANCY *walks through her routine*.

NANCY. Walks, lockstep, in and hold, turn the girl into fan,
   hockey stick, what is it, exactly? What part of me didn't...
   what part of my body?

LUKA. Nancy –

NANCY. My breasts? I know they're not...

LUKA. No.

NANCY. My teeth, my weird nose, my dad?

LUKA. No!

NANCY. My dad. It is. Tom couldn't stand him, Gary was
frightened to death of –

LUKA. Forget your dad.

NANCY. How?

Beat.

He saw me.

LUKA. He what?

NANCY. He saw me come out of your room.

LUKA. Oh.

NANCY. And don't tell me that's nothing. Just don't.

Beat.

LUKA. What did he say?

NANCY. Not a word. Never does. He just looks.

LUKA *can see* MICK *is watching*.

LUKA. I'll deal with it. I'll deal with him.

NANCY. You can't. No one can.

LUKA. I'm from Moscow.

NANCY. Luka? I thought it would help us relate. Help me
relate. In the real world, you know? Cos, all right, I met you
online but –

LUKA. I just want to dance with you, Nancy.

NANCY. It's never just dancing though, is it?

LUKA. No?

NANCY. No.

LUKA. It's Cuba.

NANCY. Cuba?

LUKA. The beaches, the blue of –

MICK. Got any batteries, son?

   LUKA *sweeps* NANCY *back into the dance.* MICK *moves towards them.*

LUKA. The Caribbean.

MICK. Do you carry 'em?

LUKA. The coffee?

NANCY. The cars.

LUKA. Walks.

NANCY. Lockstep.

LUKA. Walks –

   Lockstep –

MICK. My batteries are dead.

   MICK *goes over to* LUKA *and breaks the dance.*

LUKA. Excuse me.

MICK. You run off 'em, don't yer? Triple-As?

LUKA. Triple –

MICK. Joke. Well?

   Beat

LUKA. We don't need batteries. We don't need a camera.

MICK. This is a training tool, this.

LUKA. You're not our trainer.

MICK. No, not officially.

LUKA. No.

   Beat.

MICK. Fine. No problem. I'll just sit back, relax and be Dad.

LUKA. We'd rather you didn't.

MICK. You what?

LUKA. We'd rather you sat over there. With the spectators.

MICK. Would you, now?

LUKA. So we can focus. Prepare for the next round.

MICK. Semi-finalist? Not getting cocky now, are yer?

NANCY. Please, Dad –

MICK. 'Tis your first time in Blackpool, lad.

NANCY. Just…

> MICK *looks at* NANCY. *We hear the voice of the*
> COMPÈRE.

COMPÈRE (*voice-over*). We continue now with the final of the British National Junior Latin Championships.

MICK. Might have a look at the young 'uns. Happy memories, ey, Nance?

COMPÈRE (*voice-over*). Judging is based on all-round efficiency in the cha-cha-cha, samba, rumba…

NANCY. Happy… yes.

> *Exit* MICK.

Scene Five

Ballroom. SAMANTHA *comes out of the shadows. The* COMPÈRE*'s announcement continues but the lights turn hazy and the music takes on an ethereal quality.*

COMPÈRE (*voice-over*)....Pasodoble and jive. Thank you, adjudicators, thank you, competitors, and the very best of luck, one and all.

As the music plays, SAMANTHA *sees two* YOUNG FEMALE DANCERS.

DANCER 1 *holds out her hand to* DANCER 2. *She laughs and takes it. They partner one another, dancing purely for fun, enjoying every step of what appears to be a slow-motion routine.*

SAMANTHA *watches, as if she has conjured the memory.*

Scene Six

Ballroom. Continuous. MICK *is watching the end of the dance when* JUSTIN *approaches him.*

JUSTIN. Mick?

Takes you back, ey? The youngsters.

I was eleven when –

MICK. My gal were three.

JUSTIN. Yeah... yeah, we saw the photos.

MICK. Stood out from the off.

JUSTIN. I were sent with my sister. Dragging my heels, till I saw all the girls there and...

MICK. Pounced.

JUSTIN. Well, no, I weren't that kind of...

MICK. What?

JUSTIN. I was a limp streak of... anyway, look, I just wanted to thank you again for last night.

MICK. No need.

JUSTIN. For the chips and the beer you so kindly... Great night. I've still got a bit of an 'ead.

MICK. Not daft, am I? Nobbling the rivals. Joke, son.

JUSTIN. Oh... yeah. Ha.

MICK. My girl don't need gamesmanship, does she?

JUSTIN. Her partner's got more sense than me, I know that. Fizzy water all night.

MICK. Do you trust a man who don't drink?

JUSTIN. Well –

MICK. A Russian?

JUSTIN. Come on, Mick, they're not all... are they? You've come up trumps there, I'd say.

MICK. He has.

Awkward silence.

JUSTIN. Did I tell you last night, Mick? I've got a daughter, an' all.

MICK. With Jacqui?

JUSTIN. Jodie. And no, with my ex. She's twelve. My daughter, not... more into football than dance.

MICK. It's the way of the world.

JUSTIN. Her mother went south with her. Back to the family in Slough. I don't see her as much as I should.

MICK. And you're happy with that?

JUSTIN. Course not but...

MICK. Do summat about it, then. No buts, no bullshit. Be there.

JUSTIN. Well, I would... I want to... but me and her mum had a bust-up. Maintenance payments. See, I was sales manager, Vertigo Blinds, you know 'em?

MICK. No.

JUSTIN. Corporate work, mainly. Offices, that sort of thing. Highly competitive, just like all this. And the truth is, I took a few sick days to go to a comp. Made up the hours but you know how it is when they're looking to let people go...

MICK. You were sacked?

JUSTIN. Made redundant.

MICK. When?

JUSTIN. Two years in December. Not had a sniff of a job.

MICK. And Jacqui?

JUSTIN. Jodie. She works for a cleaning firm. Upmarket houses, like yours. Fits in with this but it's hard in the current... austerity, you know, to...

MICK. What?

JUSTIN. And when you were saying last night, you've that big new development starting up... eight B&Bs into flats.

MICK. Apartments.

JUSTIN. Well, Mick, I was wondering... do you need blokes on the site?

MICK. Doing?

JUSTIN. Anything. Labouring.

MICK. You?

JUSTIN. I'm fit. Well, I am once my knee's… I'm willing and able, I'll work for an hourly rate.

MICK. You're management, Justin. You reek of it.

JUSTIN. I'm a competitive dancer. All right, an amateur dancer –

MICK. That's a rank not a judgement.

JUSTIN. See? You know what it means, you know what it is. You know that to stay in the game, you can't keep a full-time job down. You need flexible hours, you need…

MICK. Minimum wage. Can you do this on that?

JUSTIN. I've twenty-six pounds in my wallet, Mick. Twenty-six pounds left, that's all.

MICK *takes a few moments to consider the thought.*

MICK. I might have a job for you.

JUSTIN. Honest? Well, that's –

MICK. Just say yes or no –

JUSTIN. Yes –

MICK. And don't speak about it again.

Beat.

JUSTIN. What kind of job?

MICK. Semi-final.

JUSTIN. What semi-final?

MICK. The one coming up. When you're out there, just give him a nice little elbow to throw him off-track.

JUSTIN. Sorry, give who…?

MICK. Rasputin.

JUSTIN. Now, hang on. We don't know we're through yet, we don't know they're through.

MICK. You've both done enough. He's done more than enough. So we just need to break him in, show him who's boss.

JUSTIN. Break him in?

MICK. She thinks he's a stallion. Make him look like a carthorse tonight.

Beat.

JUSTIN. You're saying you want me to nobble him?

MICK. I'm saying accidents happen. You know that. Broken strides, broken ribs. One thousand pounds, cash in hand.

JUSTIN. A grand...

MICK. Gets your car back on the road. A nice little treat for the wife.

JUSTIN *thinks for a few moments.*

JUSTIN. Thank you.

MICK. Don't mention it. Ever. That's the deal.

JUSTIN. Thank you for making me see what an arse I've become.

MICK. Oh?

JUSTIN. Cos for a moment there... Christ! I would have, I could have...

MICK. Are you saying no?

JUSTIN. Yes. No. I'm saying No Way.

MICK *looks at* JUSTIN.

MICK. You're not an arse. You're a loser.

JUSTIN. Am I? We'll see.

Scene Seven

Atherton Corner. Later that evening. JODIE is warming up, contorting herself into weird and wonderful shapes. SAMANTHA watches her, water bottle in hand.

SAMANTHA. Excuse me? Sorry.

   JODIE turns around to see SAMANTHA.

JODIE. Oh.

SAMANTHA. I've mislaid my hairspray, I don't suppose…

JODIE. There's a Boots outside.

SAMANTHA. I've mislaid the outside.

JODIE. You've…

SAMANTHA. Hello.

JODIE. Whatever.

SAMANTHA. Would you mind?

   JODIE reluctantly throws her a can of hairspray.

JODIE. Not if you're quick.

SAMANTHA. You're too kind.

JODIE. No, I'm not. Do it here and get gone.

   SAMANTHA sprays her hair and the soles of her shoes.

SAMANTHA. I'd lose my head if it wasn't sprayed on. I'd go up in a big cloud of lacquer.

JODIE. I'm sure.

SAMANTHA. Lacquer. I like that word, don't you? Lacquered. I'm lacquered. Thank you.

   SAMANTHA looks at JODIE a little woozily.

JODIE. What's up?

SAMANTHA. *Comment allez-vous?*

JODIE. It's rude to stare.

SAMANTHA. Jodie –

JODIE. It's rude.

SAMANTHA. Do you remember?

JODIE. Don't have time, duck.

> JODIE *takes the hairspray.*

SAMANTHA. The Penny Black School of Dance. Four nights a week. Church hall, strip lights, ice on the windows, inside. Twenty-odd girls, very odd, some of them, vying for two little boys. Medals and minivans, glitter-spray, cheap plastic trophies –

JODIE. They weren't cheap to me.

> *Beat.*

SAMANTHA. We *were* partners, weren't we? I haven't just dreamt it all up?

> *Beat.*

JODIE. Yeah. For a bit. Cos there weren't enough lads to go round.

SAMANTHA. I was eleven. You were –

JODIE. Your nanny.

SAMANTHA. You were, in a way.

JODIE. At comps and –

SAMANTHA. I looked up to you.

JODIE. Well, you didn't have a choice. I was a foot taller than you were, back then.

SAM. 'Footwork, flooring, music. That's all it is, girls. Three little words: footwork, flooring – '

JODIE. Sam, what do you want?

SAM. 'Rise and fall, rise and fall, rise and fall,' remember? 'Up the hills, down the valleys.'

JODIE. I remember you dumped me for Alistair Blunt.

SAMANTHA. Did I?

JODIE. You dumped me and never looked back.

Beat.

SAMANTHA. She was ambitious. Penny.

JODIE. And you weren't?

SAMANTHA. You tell me? Jodie? Tell me what I was like?

JODIE *looks at* SAMANTHA.

JODIE. Funny.

SAMANTHA. What kind of funny?

JODIE. Look, all I know is… yeah, I'd have binned you if Bluntly had asked but I wouldn't have blanked you from that moment on. Cos… cos we did all right, you and me.

SAMANTHA. I know.

JODIE. We had a laugh. We won stuff. And I'm not saying you wouldn't have made it wi'out me, you would. Course you would. But I think I did help you a bit. Early days, with the little stuff –

SAMANTHA. Big stuff. I'm sorry.

Beat.

JODIE. Don't be. It's over and done with.

SAMANTHA. I'm not sure it is, quite. For me.

JODIE. Yeah, well… I'm sorry, an' all. 'Bout your mum. Cos I heard what she went through… and you too. I wanted to send you a card or…

SAMANTHA. I still go out there expecting to see her. Front row. Sat in her favourite seat. Glowering.

JODIE. You shouldn't speak ill of the dead.

SAMANTHA. Why not? She did.

JODIE. Well, that's true, and the living.

SAMANTHA. Penny spoke ill of just about everyone.

JODIE. Why don't you call her Mum?

SAMANTHA. Never have. Never did. Nepotism: so she wasn't accused of, you know? When she picked me above...

JODIE. Me.

SAMANTHA. Is that what she did? What I did?

Beat.

JODIE. You had a lot to put up with, I know.

SAMANTHA. Oh... it wasn't all bad?

JODIE. I know. But when you look back, quite a lot of it was.

Beat.

SAMANTHA. Except the aquarium.

JODIE. Bloody hell, that!

SAMANTHA. You remember?

JODIE. How can I forget? It took up the whole entire room.

SAMANTHA. Do you remember your favourite? Tiger barbs, angelfish, mollies?

JODIE. That fat ugly thing on the bottom that ate all the crap.

SAMANTHA. The one we called Graham?

JODIE. After my stepdad –

SAMANTHA. Oh, yes!

JODIE. That's him! Yeah... that was him...

A reflective silence.

SAMANTHA. So how is it? Slater Street?

JODIE. Oh, the same.

SAMANTHA. You're still there?

JODIE. Three streets down.

SAMANTHA. And all the old haunts, are they...?

JODIE. Older. Haunted. Feels like a ghost town.

SAMANTHA. But if I were to come down one day...

JODIE. Don't.

SAMANTHA. If I were to come, would you... could we perhaps take a walk and a... could we?

COMPÈRE (*voice-over*). And now we continue with the semi-final of the Amateur Latin Championship.

JUSTIN *crosses to* JODIE.

JUSTIN. Jodie!

JODIE. What?

JUSTIN. We're going out there. Whether they call us or not.

JODIE. You what?

SAMANTHA. Jodie?

Enter LEE, *urgently.*

LEE. Samantha, I thought you'd...

COMPÈRE (*voice-over*). Fourteen couples are recalled and they are: numbers 16, 22 –

JUSTIN. Jodie? We're on.

COMPÈRE (*voice-over*). 27, 29 –

JODIE *looks at* SAMANTHA.

JODIE. Yeah. Come.

JUSTIN. We're on.

JUSTIN *puts out his arm.* JODIE *takes it and they walk, smiling, to the dance floor.*

COMPÈRE (*voice-over*). 35, 38, 42, 44, 51, 55, 60, 71, 73
    and 75.

LUKA. Cha-cha-cha?

NANCY. Cha-cha-cha.

LUKA *and* NANCY *trot onto the dance floor, leaving* LEE
    and SAMANTHA *alone*.

LEE. Out.

SAMANTHA. Out.

Scene Eight

Dance floor. Continuous. JUSTIN *and* JODIE, NANCY *and*
LUKA *join members of the* DANCE CHORUS *for the Latin
semi-final.*

COMPÈRE (*voice-over*). Competitors, your first dance, the cha-
    cha-cha.

*With bright Cuban rhythms and highly synchronised moves,
the flirtatious Brazilian party dance sees the dancers going
all out for Latin glory.*

*The couples dance in unison, with great bounce and rolls,
their bodies rotating together. As the cha-cha-cha changes to
the samba, the semi-final ends with a snap.*

Scene Nine

Hart/Shaw Dressing Room. Later that evening. LEE is taking off his costume. SAMANTHA's bags are packed.

LEE. Out in the quarters.

SAMANTHA. It happens.

LEE. Not to me.

Beat.

SAMANTHA. There's no way back from this, is there?

LEE. No.

SAMANTHA. No.

Beat.

LEE. We'll tell the sponsors it's labyrinthitis. Dizziness, vertigo. Goes on for months sometimes. Years.

SAMANTHA. Labyrinthi...

LEE. Except you need to be sober to say it.

SAMANTHA. Thank you.

LEE. It's for my reputation, not yours.

SAMANTHA. Of course. Worry not. I'll keep... mum.

LEE looks up.

LEE. See someone. A doctor. Go somewhere.

SAMANTHA. I will. I want to. I thought perhaps the Pleasure Beach?

LEE. Fine.

LEE continues to pack.

SAMANTHA. All these years I've been coming to Blackpool: no candyfloss, no 'Kiss Me Quick' hats.

LEE. Kiss Me Quickstep.

SAMANTHA. No sea horses. They mate for life, did you know?

LEE. Not in the Irish Sea.

SAMANTHA. Lee? Will you do that, do you think? Mate for life? Would you like to?

LEE. That's very kind of you. No.

SAMANTHA. You can even get married now, can't you?

LEE. I know.

SAMANTHA. The world's changed. The real world, anyhow.

LEE. This is my world.

SAMANTHA. But is it enough, Lee?

LEE. It's more than enough. It's more than I ever thought possible.

SAMANTHA. Oh?

Beat.

LEE. I was shy as a boy. I was fey. But dance gave me – made me – helped me express myself. Let me say things I'd never have spoken aloud.

SAMANTHA. I think it's silenced me. Bound and gagged.

LEE. I'd have been nothing without it. No one. I'd be sat in a call centre somewhere. 'Hello, this is Lee here from Nowhere.' Going quietly out of my mind.

Beat.

SAMANTHA. We should take a walk on the pier.

LEE. It's November.

SAMANTHA. Blow away all the cobwebs, the phantoms.

LEE. It won't help your labyrinthitis.

SAMANTHA. Sorry, my?

LEE. Labyrinth–

SAMANTHA. Makes you deaf. Bu-bum.

LEE. You're not funny.

SAMANTHA. But I could be. I could be anything now.

LEE. You're Samantha Shaw. Number One, ballroom and Latin.

SAMANTHA. I was, yes.

> SAMANTHA *gives her water bottle to* LEE.
>
> I was.

Scene Ten

Knight Corner. Later that night. LUKA *and* NANCY *are devising a new samba routine.*

LUKA. Basic samba step and –

NANCY. One, and two, and three, and four.

LUKA. And whisk, and whisk and whisk and whisk –

NANCY. And promenade. Walks.

LUKA. And two, and three cross-through-and-cross-and-turn; cross-and-turn; cross-and-turn; cross-and-turn.

NANCY. Promenade walks. And two and three and four.

LUKA. And botafogo, cross, two, three and four.

NANCY. And turn in volta, and volta, and volta and close.

> MICK *comes in, with* NANCY*'s luggage.*

LUKA. Yes, yes, yes. Now let's break that down.

MICK. Break it down? You're done.

NANCY *and* LUKA *run through the figures, watched by* MICK.

LUKA. Basic samba step – and one, and two, and three, and four.

MICK. Don't bother, you're out.

NANCY. Who says?

LUKA *and* NANCY *repeat the figure.*

LUKA. Basic... and one, and two, and three, and four.

MICK. A samba needs bounce.

NANCY. That's what we're working on, Dad.

MICK. Your rumba? Head problems.

LUKA. And promenade. Walks –

MICK. Cha-cha-cha: reasonable balance, fluidity, rhythm. Paso lacked a Spanish line. Jive? You'd not practised.

NANCY. We're practising now.

LUKA. Walks –

NANCY. Right...

LUKA. And two, and three cross-through-and-cross-and turn; cross and turn; cross and turn; cross and turn.

NANCY. Promenade walks.

LUKA. And two, and three, and –

NANCY. Oops –

MICK. You're tired, see? Home time.

LUKA. We are not ready to go.

NANCY. We're not out yet.

MICK. I saw you dancing. I say you are.

LUKA. Mr Knight, you're not helping –

MICK. Not helping with what? Your airfare, your visa? Your private lessons, your Supadance shoes, your handmade suit?

LUKA. We made an arrangement.

MICK. I made an investment, in you. I pulled strings. And I hope for your sake, you're not pulling mine.

LUKA. Excuse me. We have work to do.

LUKA *turns back to* NANCY.

MICK. Work? Don't you tell me about work.

LUKA. Nancy?

MICK. Labourer, bricklayer, foreman, contractor, that's me.

NANCY. And one, and two, and three, and four –

MICK. Built a house, sold it, built three. Sold 'em, built six. Sold 'em, built twelve. Twenty. Fifty-five. So it goes on. Local councillor. Prospective mayor –

LUKA. Sorry, what's this to do with our samba?

MICK. I make things happen, Luke.

LUKA. Luka.

MICK. I made all this happen, for Nancy. I made her a junior champion.

LUKA. She made herself. And I dance with your daughter, not you.

MICK *grabs hold of* LUKA.

MICK. Oh, you do, do you?

NANCY. Dad…

MICK. In my house?

MICK *reaches down and squeezes his testicles, hard.* LUKA *cries out in pain and falls to the floor.*

NANCY. Dad, for God's sake!

MICK. From Russia with love.

LUKA. *Bozhe moi.*

NANCY. It's the Juvenile Nationals all over again.

    NANCY *goes to* LUKA.

MICK. Leave him.

NANCY. No –

MICK. Leave. Him.

NANCY. No! Not this time. No.

MICK. Nancy, we're going home.

NANCY. You're going home.

MICK. Don't you tell me –

NANCY. Go now. Now!

MICK. Not without you, come on.

NANCY. I told you, no!

    MICK *gets hold of* NANCY *but she pulls away.*

    I'll come when I'm ready. And then…

MICK. What?

NANCY. I'll pack a bag. Get a room.

MICK. With him?

NANCY. Without you.

    Beat.

MICK. I see.

NANCY. But you don't, you don't see it at all.

MICK. Well, what have I missed, ey? What am I meant to be…

    Beat.

NANCY. Me.

Beat.

MICK. Nancy, I fed you, I clothed you, I've nurtured you since –

NANCY. I know that! I know, but...

MICK. What? What!

NANCY. I just want to be on my own for... that's all.

Beat.

MICK. Don't go to her. Swear you won't go to your –

NANCY. Dad, stop this –

MICK. She left you, remember that. High and dry.

NANCY. No, she left you. She lost me.

MICK. You were much better off. You didn't know her, see? Not like I did.

NANCY. Cos I didn't have the chance to.

MICK. Nancy, this isn't the place for –

NANCY. You're right. So please? Go home.

MICK. But it's not home wi'out...

NANCY. I can't help that, Dad. Go.

MICK *looks at* NANCY *and sees she means it. Exit* MICK.

LUKA *moves sympathetically towards* NANCY.

LUKA. Nancy –

NANCY. I'm not crying. I'm not.

Exit NANCY.

Scene Eleven

Atherton Corner. Continuous. JUSTIN *has his trouser leg rolled up.* JODIE *is applying ice cubes.*

JODIE. He's a nutter.

JUSTIN. I know.

JODIE. He actually asked you to go out and...?

JUSTIN. Break a rib.

JODIE. He's a total nutter.

JUSTIN. And I'm a prize idiot, too.

JODIE. You're a hero, Justin. You did the right thing when you could have...

JUSTIN. A thousand pounds... drop in the ocean, in't it?

JODIE. You're a hero.

   JODIE *applies the ice pack harder.*

JUSTIN. Ow!

JODIE. Oh, shut up, you'll live.

JUSTIN. That's what I'm worried about.

JODIE. What do you mean?

JUSTIN. It's a mess, Jo. A massive big mess.

JODIE. Yes, all right, the codeine don't work.

JUSTIN. Not me knee.

JODIE. The pasodoble was paso-don't-ble.

JUSTIN. I'm talking life not dance. We've got to go home now. We've got to get work.

JODIE. We're working at this.

JUSTIN. Real work. Jobs. Careers with a salary, overtime, pension. We've got to stop living in La-La-Land.

JODIE. Burslem.

JUSTIN. We've got to stop.

Beat.

JODIE. Stop dancing?

JUSTIN. If that's what it takes.

JODIE. But Justin, we're good. We're better than ever, we're right on the brink.

JUSTIN. Brink of ruin.

JODIE. We're not giving up. I'm not giving up.

JUSTIN. I'm not asking you to. Cos you're bang-on, you're right. We're at the top of our game. We're as good as it gets, as good as it's gonna get. This is the peak of the mountain. The time to retire.

JODIE. I'm not even thirty.

JUSTIN. You see? You can go out on top. Here, tonight. Think about it.

JODIE. Retire and do what?

JUSTIN. Pay off our debts. Start again with the ordinary things.

JODIE. We're not ordinary.

JUSTIN. I am. I just want a job and a house and a baby and you.

JODIE. Hang on –

JUSTIN. Weekends at home with the telly on, walking the dog.

JODIE. What baby? What dog?

JUSTIN. When we're settled and straight. Why not?

Beat.

JODIE. A baby? You've had one.

JUSTIN. Perhaps I'd like two. Three. Four, when we're sorted.

JODIE. Why haven't you said so before?

JUSTIN. I have. You don't listen.

JODIE. Oh, I see, so it's my fault –

JUSTIN. It's nobody's fault but you've got to face up to this, Jodie. We live like professional dancers who aren't getting paid. And we can't any more, can we?

JODIE. You want me to give up my whole entire life?

JUSTIN. Aren't I your life?

JODIE. You're my husband, my partner, my... but I was a dancer before you and...

COMPÈRE (*voice-over*). Thank you, competitors. Thank you, adjudicators. We continue now with the final of Amateur Latin.

JUSTIN. And?

COMPÈRE (*voice-over*). Eight couples are recalled and they are: number 16, 22, 29, 35, 38, 42, 51, 71.

JODIE. Listen...

JUSTIN. We're living in Neverland, Jodie.

JODIE. We're through.

JUSTIN. That's what I'm saying –

JODIE. Through to the final.

JUSTIN. You and me?

JODIE *offers her hand to* JUSTIN.

JODIE. My husband. My partner?

JUSTIN *takes* JODIE*'s hand and they go to the dance floor.*

Scene Twelve

Dance floor. Continuous. JUSTIN *shows off his partner.* JODIE *soaks up the applause. The atmosphere is electric, with shouts of 'Come on, Number 29' and 'Number 42' from all four corners of the ballroom. The* DANCE CHORUS *line the ballroom, adding to the sense of occasion.*

COMPÈRE (*voice-over*). Cha-cha-cha!

The music begins. Alone, JUSTIN *and* JODIE *are in perfect harmony as they deliver the synchronised movements of the dance.*

Samba!

JUSTIN *and* JODIE *bounce, roll and rotate as if their life depends on it. The cheering and applause intensifies as one dance segues into another.*

Rumba!

The music segues into the sensual Latin dance, with JODIE *using all her power and charm to dominate* JUSTIN. *As part of the romantic dance, they deliver forward and backward walks, and exquisite spot turns.*

Pasodoble!

JUSTIN *relishes the role of the toreador,* JODIE *the cappa. It is a riot of flamenco foot-stamping, marching movements and flamboyant hand gestures as the competing couple battle it out. Both push their performance up a gear, finding every element of drama in the angry sexuality of the antagonistic dance.*

And your fifth and final dance, competitors: the jive.

The music segues and the mood changes into an American 1930s dancehall. The speed of the dancing increases and the movements are sharp as a knife. It is a riot of competitive kicks, flicks and spins.

The jive brings the final to an exuberant climax. JUSTIN *and* JODIE *take their final bow, to cheers, whistles and wild applause.*

Scene Thirteen

Atherton Corner. Continuous. A breathless JUSTIN *and* JODIE*'s shoulders and smiles fall. We hear the now-distant voice of the* COMPÈRE.

COMPÈRE (*voice-over*). Thank you, competitors, thank you, adjudicators. What a spectacle that was! Dancing of the highest order. Thank you!

JUSTIN. 'Dance like there's nobody watching.' Who said that, I wonder?

JODIE. Like nobody's watching? Why would yer?

JUSTIN. But for a moment out there…

JODIE. It did.

Beat.

JUSTIN. What if we sell the house? Clear the debts. Downsize.

JODIE. From a two-bedroom terrace?

JUSTIN. I'd live with you in a cardboard box.

JODIE. Don't say that, you might have to.

JUSTIN. We'll give it a year. One more year.

JODIE. Do you mean that?

JUSTIN. Full-time, full-on. Use what we make on the house to support us.

JODIE. Won't be much.

JUSTIN. Might be enough to turn pro?

JODIE. You and me?

JUSTIN. Why not, if we're dancing like that? If we knuckle down. If I knuckle down.

JODIE. And you want to? You honestly want to?

JUSTIN (*as Winston Churchill*). 'This is not the end. This is not even the beginning of the end. This is just perhaps the end of the beginning.'

JODIE. What are you saying it like that for?

JUSTIN. I'm Churchill.

JODIE. The dog?

JUSTIN. The Prime Minister.

JODIE. What did he know about dance?

JUSTIN. Nowt, but we do. Bloody hell, Jodie, we do.

COMPÈRE (*voice-over*). And now we come to that point of the evening we're all looking forward to: the results of the British Amateur Latin American Championship.

JODIE. Oh God.

JUSTIN *and* JODIE *pick themselves up and prepare.*

JUSTIN. It's all right, it's fine. If we're not placed this time, we've got summat to build on.

JODIE. A personal best.

JUSTIN. I'll say.

JODIE. We can take it away, the experience.

JUSTIN. Take it and work it and…

JUSTIN *takes* JODIE'*s hand.*

COMPÈRE (*voice-over*). Into first place, by being placed first in the cha-cha-cha, the rumba, the pasadoble and second in the samba and the jive: from Ipswich, Number 35, Darrell and Romily Fry!

Applause and fanfare.

JUSTIN. Darrell and Romily, fair play.

COMPÈRE (*voice-over*). Into second place: from Deal, Number 71, Ian Swan and Jayne Russell-Jones.

JODIE. How the hell have they –

JUSTIN. Claws in, please.

Applause and fanfare.

COMPÈRE (*voice-over*). Into third place: from Stoke-on-Trent, Number 22, Justin and Jodie Atherton.

JODIE. Justin and...

JUSTIN. Third?

Applause and fanfare.

JODIE. Third!

With a flamboyant turn, JUSTIN *and* JODIE *are on the dance floor. There are cheers, whoops and flashbulbs. They take an elaborate bow separately and then together.*

JUSTIN *presents* JODIE *to the audience, to great acclaim. He receives a trophy, she a bouquet. They pose for flash photographers, their smiles as wide as Blackpool front.*

Scene Fourteen

Dance floor. End of the night. A CLEANER *sweeps the floor. A handful of* DANCERS *are warming down, packing up, saying goodbye.*

Enter SAMANTHA, *with her bags. She crosses the dance floor, stops, crouches down and puts the palm of her hand gently on the floor.* LEE *is watching her.*

LEE. So this is it?

SAMANTHA. Yep. 'It.'

LEE. No tears, no valediction.

SAMANTHA. No. Just The End.

LEE. Well, not quite. There's the rest of your life.

SAMANTHA. Oh, yes… that.

LEE. You'll teach, I suppose?

SAMANTHA. I don't think so.

LEE. What else do you know? Except fish.

SAMANTHA. There's a chippy down the road with a card in the window. They need a fryer.

LEE. There's Sea World.

SAMANTHA. Strange exotic creatures? Seen 'em all.

LEE. Sam? When you've found yourself, do let me know who you are. I might like her better, who knows?

SAMANTHA *bows, as* LEE *would at the end of a routine.* LEE *looks at her and gives a respectful nod.*

SAMANTHA. Rise and fall.

LEE. Oh, I will.

SAMANTHA. Rise.

Exit SAMANTHA, *to a new life. She crosses with* NANCY, *carrying her own bags. She stops to reorganise her luggage in a more manageable way.*

LEE. Can I help?

NANCY. Thank you, I'm fine.

LEE *watches her struggle with her luggage.*

LEE. Marvellous work tonight. Marvellous paso.

NANCY. Thank you.

NANCY *picks up her luggage and goes to leave.*

LEE. Lee Hart.

NANCY. I know.

LEE. I was saying, your paso. Tremendous conviction.

NANCY. Thanks.

LEE. With your core strength and passion, you really are...

NANCY. Strong. Passionate.

LEE. Quite.

NANCY. Well, I try.

NANCY *sets off towards the exit. As she does,* LUKA *comes in, also carrying his bag.*

LEE. The 106 Dance School, d'you know it?

NANCY. In Manchester?

LEE. Monday. Midday. Shall we meet?

NANCY. Why?

LEE. I'd like us to try out, that's all.

NANCY. Try out?

LEE. Why not? You're good. You've got the poise, the posture, the smoothness, the breath of the movement.

NANCY. But Samantha's...

LEE. We've come to the end of the rainbow. That's Blackpool. More couples break up here than at Christmas.

NANCY *glances at* LUKA, *who stands out of* LEE*'s sight.*

NANCY. This was our first competition. My partner and I.

LEE. And as I say, you danced well. But may I be frank?

NANCY. Frank? I thought you were Lee?

LEE. You don't have the power to truly be moving together: to drive through the feet. To soften or strengthen the movement.

NANCY. Has Dad put you up to this?

LEE. Dad?

NANCY. My dad.

LEE. My darling, do I give a damn for anyone's 'dad'?

NANCY. I doubt it, no.

LEE. 106. Monday. Midday.

LEE *gives* NANCY *his card.*

LUKA. Nancy?

NANCY *turns to* LUKA.

NANCY. You'll find a room tonight?

LUKA. As you say: vacancies.

NANCY. You've got the cash to...

LUKA. A little. Enough.

Beat.

NANCY. Did you just come for the money?

LUKA. The –

NANCY. Money. Are you partnering me cos he –

LUKA. No.

NANCY. Cos I'd understand if you were. I mean…

LUKA. I came here to try out with you. And we…

NANCY. Clicked.

LEE. Cute.

LUKA. We did. We do.

    NANCY *looks at* LUKA, *weighing him up.*

NANCY. So what are you doing tomorrow?

LUKA. Perhaps, maybe, go to the Tower.

NANCY. You've not seen it yet, have you?

LUKA. Except on TV.

NANCY. Perhaps, maybe, I'll meet you there?

LUKA. Yes?

NANCY. Two o'clock. Bring your Supadance shoes.

LUKA. Right…

NANCY. Our samba needs work. Our rumba, our paso.

    LEE *plucks his card from* NANCY's *hand.*

LEE. You win some, you lose some.

NANCY. And then…

LUKA. And then…

NANCY. One day at a time, ey? Tomorrow.

    Exit NANCY. LUKA *turns to* LEE.

LUKA. No power, huh?

LEE. What I meant was –

LUKA. I know what you meant. And it's true. But we will.

LEE. Well…

   LEE *turns to go.*

LUKA. Back home, you know… the street I grow up in – no money, no work – the future for young men is crime, is drugs, is… but me, I'm lucky. I'm different. I have a way out.

LEE. And here you are.

LUKA. Luka. Luka Kralj.

LEE. Lee –

LUKA. I know who you are. You've got the poise, the posture.

LEE. Ha-ha.

LUKA. You're what I came here to see. To be.

LEE. You're too kind.

   Beat.

LUKA. Wanna go boogie?

LEE. Boogie?

LUKA. Out there.

LEE. Not tonight.

LUKA. Yes, tonight! I come six thousand miles and my feet are on fire.

   LUKA *does a disco step. As he looks at* LEE, *an understanding passes between them.*

LEE. Where are you from?

LUKA. Moscow.

LEE. Is it as bad over there as they say?

LUKA. It's worse.

   Beat.

LEE. I do know a club.

LUKA. Show me.

LEE. Really? Now?

LUKA. What else do we have but the now?

LEE *smiles*.

LEE. Oh, this town...

LUKA *gives a nod to the ballroom*.

LUKA. Blackpool.

Scene Fifteen

Dance floor. Finale. Music. The DANCE CHORUS *launch a dance medley of ballroom and Latin, with our three couples joining them, dancing freely with one another.*

MICK *takes the place of the* COMPÈRE, *introducing each couple in the closing bows. The show ends in the spirit of a ballroom and Latin carnival.*

The End.

A Nick Hern Book

Kiss Me Quickstep first published in Great Britain as a paperback original in 2016 by Nick Hern Books Limited, The Glasshouse, 49a Goldhawk Road, London W12 8QP, in association with the New Vic Theatre and Oldham Coliseum Theatre

Kiss Me Quickstep copyright © 2016 Amanda Whittington

Amanda Whittington has asserted her right to be identified as the author of this work

Cover image: Getty Images
Cover design: Candida Kelsall

Designed and typeset by Nick Hern Books, London
Printed in Great Britain by CPI Group (UK) Ltd

A CIP catalogue record for this book is available from the British Library

ISBN 978 1 84842 518 7

CAUTION   All rights whatsoever in this play are strictly reserved. Requests to reproduce the text in whole or in part should be addressed to the publisher.

Amateur Performing Rights   Applications for performance, including readings and excerpts, in the English language throughout the world by amateurs should be addressed to the Performing Rights Manager, Nick Hern Books, The Glasshouse, 49a Goldhawk Road, London W12 8QP, *tel* +44 (0)20 8749 4953, *e-mail* rights@nickhernbooks.co.uk, except as follows:

Australia: Dominie Drama, 8 Cross Street, Brookvale 2100, *tel* (+2) 9938 8686, *fax* (2) 9938 8695, *e-mail* drama@dominie.com.au

New Zealand: Play Bureau, PO Box 420, New Plymouth, *tel* (+6) 757 3103, *e-mail* info@playbureau.com

South Africa: DALRO (pty) Ltd, PO Box 31627, 2017 Braamfontein, *tel* (11) 712 8000, *fax* (11) 403 9094, *e-mail* theatricals@dalro.co.za

United States of America and Canada: Alan Brodie Representation Ltd, see details below

Professional Performing Rights   Applications for performance by professionals in any medium and in any language throughout the world (and by amateur and stock companies in the United States of America and Canada) should be addressed to the Alan Brodie Representation Ltd, Paddock Suite, The Courtyard, 55a Charterhouse Street, London EC1M 6HA, *fax* +44 (0)20 7183 7999, *e-mail* info@alanbrodie.com

No performance of any kind may be given unless a licence has been obtained. Applications should be made before rehearsals begin. Publication of this play does not necessarily indicate its availability for performance.